Black, Blanc, Beur

Rap Music and Hip-Hop Culture in the Francophone World

Edited by Alain-Philippe Durand

The Scarecrow Press, Inc.
Lanham, Maryland, and Oxford
2002

ML
3531
.B52
2002
cop.2
JAZZ

SCARECROW PRESS, INC.

Published in the United States of America
by Scarecrow Press, Inc.
A Member of the Rowman & Littlefield Publishing Group
4720 Boston Way, Lanham, Maryland 20706
www.scarecrowpress.com

PO Box 317
Oxford
OX2 9RU, UK

British Library Cataloguing in Publication Information Available

Library of Congress Cataloging-in-Publication Data

Black, blanc, beur : rap music and hip-hop culture in the francophone
world / edited by Alain-Philippe Durand.
       p. cm.
Includes bibliographical references and index
  ISBN 0-8108-4430-3 (cloth : alk. paper) — ISBN 0-8108-4431-1 (pbk. :
alk. paper)
  1. Rap (Music)—France—History and criticism. 2. Rap (Music)—Quebec
  (Province)—History and criticism. 3. Rap (Music)—Gabon—History and
criticism. I. Durand, Alain-Philippe
  ML3531 .B52 2002
  782.421649'0944—dc21

                                                            2002007050

B 2017003

Pour l'équipe d'animation: Lionel, Michel, et Patrick
Pour Théo

"Je sais que tu peux"

—Sidney

IN MEMORIAM

André J. M. Prévos
(1948–2002)

Contents

Foreword:
Francophone Hip-Hop as a Colonial Urban Geography

Adam Krims

One of the more remarkable facts about this collection is that it should be the first one published of scholarly studies on French (and Francophone) hip-hop. It is almost, if not fully, a truism among hip-hop fans that France is second only to the United States in the venerability of its scenes, the cultural influence of hip-hop, and its sophistication in the evolution of new artistic forms and cultural practices. The French hip-hop scene was already legendary, in fact, when I became a rap fan in the late 1980s, long before I finally made it to Marseilles to attend their renowned annual festival. And even those Anglophone consumers who have only seen *La Haine* and heard MC Solaar on a college radio station or in the local café seem to realize that they are witnessing the tip of a social iceberg, the power of a social movement that, like so much vernacular art in France and its sometimes former colonies, is felt intensely throughout the society, opposed as vigorously as it is loved. Hip-hop fans and artists worldwide—MCs, DJs, b-boys and b-girls, and taggers—have been unable to ignore the force of hip-hop culture from the Francophone world, but why did a book as important as this take so long? Part of the reason is assuredly one I have voiced before (Krims), namely the fixation of rap and hip-hop scholars on the United States; to be fair, mapping the cultural force even of American hip-hop was a project that imposed itself on the academic world only after rap music had already imprinted itself on the society for more than a decade. What is more, the long-missing attention to hip-hop culture outside the United States is now starting to rear its head (Mitchell; Krims), promising perhaps a growth industry like that for American rap scholarship in the

1990s. But one might have thought, given some of the theoretical predilections of the past decade or so, that Francophone hip-hop culture should have suggested itself as a privileged object for cultural studies: what better models hybridity, identity formation, liminality, cultural resistance, the deformation and reformation of black (and many other) masculinities? Only somewhat ironically, in France itself several distinguished studies have already emerged (e.g., Bazin; Milon), where such theoretical fixations are less prevalent.

Never mind. The present collection plows a terrain that anybody who was paying attention knew was immeasurably rich, and it goes a long way toward suggesting how the worlds of Francophone expressive vernacular culture map both a totality and their own particularity. Far from the shopworn notion of hip-hop as quintessential urban guerilla practice, the essays collected here allow for subtle mappings of the intertwined structures of urban form, cultural production, class, and ethnicity. The twisted braids of those social forces then multiply themselves as the focus extends from France itself to cities in Africa and North America—in which the paths of cultural transit not only double back on themselves but also cross into, and back from, regions well outside the Francophone world. In Libreville, for example, the presence of both the colonial language and post-colonial media are mediated through local ethnic, tribal, and urban-spatial (e.g., neighborhood) affiliations; while in Quebec, the differentiation among colonially associated subjects by "race" is mediated by its situation in North America and inflection by anglophone (principally American) media culture. The result, a peculiar imbrication of "white" scopophilia to a population already on the linguistic defense, could only be possible in that unique meeting of anglophone and Francophone colonial geographies. Thus, the borders of the Francophone colonial world (and surely it is not yet "post-colonial") continually blur, while that world's Atlantic nexus of exchange retains, and reinflects, a character established over the centuries. Neither the rhetorical sinkhole of "hybridity" nor the free-market slogan of "globalization" captures this dynamic, but the essays gathered here at least begin to suggest it.

In the meantime, the old tag of hip-hop as the quintessential "urban" culture—though it obscures the more intimate imbrication of most or all mass-musics with public perceptions of urban life—can nevertheless yield substantial fruit, taken the right way. The implication of urban structure, spaces objective and subjective, with the development and impact of hip-hop culture link each essay; and following the expressive forms backward into those urban spaces can form the beginnings of a complex mapping of the economic/cultural contours of contemporary Francophone cities. The devastated agglomerations of misery in the *cités* (housing projects) of Paris and Marseilles form at the same time localized economic peripheries and hip-hop cores for all of France, if not the Francophone world overall; their particular place and ethnic identities then are constructed and coded within the expressive poetics of music, dance, and graffiti. The first eight essays in the collection together map that process, across media and across France, anchored in Paris and Marseilles but extending to Toulon and Orange in the infamous "affaire NTM." Lyon, interestingly, makes its appearance only in the medium of dance, along with a peculiar and refreshing mutual permeability between the authenticities of "the street" and the world of commercial production. The dissemination of such expressive codings through the urban networks of a culture industry, or transport systems, then insure their mingling with far-flung cities already implicated in long-standing colonial interchanges. Those urban recipients may either host their own *cités* or, indeed, function more as generalized subordinate spaces to the originating colonial center; in either case, the subsequent representations—and yes, inflections—of those other urban structures in new expressive poetics reinscribe in sound and vision a new metropolitan division of labor (Scott) and spatial organization; the final two essays afford a glimpse of those processes. Given the infinite and rapid accumulation of such recursive inscriptions, not to mention the free reversibility of each process, it is probably tempting, at some point in reading these essays, to give up any determinate spatial mappings and succumb to a more properly postmodern celebration of their final hybridity—or almost equivalently, to celebrate hip-hop's purported resistance to any force of dominant cultural containment. Such a response, though, would be unnecessary and, worse, would betray the opportunity to see hip-hop culture and urban spaces as two faces of the same processes, mutually conditioning and determining. Those two faces would not necessarily be mutually mappable as homologies; but their inseparable mutual implication could easily suggest the profound error of conceiving of "the economic" and "the cultural" as separate spheres, thereafter posing as a problem their (thenceforth impossible) reconciliation. This is the lesson taught to us by Derek Sayer about Marx's notion of the dialectic, and its fallout for the old problem of base and superstructure. What is perhaps most impressive about the essays assembled by Alain-Philippe Durand, even more so than presenting to the anglophone world scholars heretofore known mainly to Francophone academia, is the ease with which the essays weave paths that suggest that very dialectic, always in the fractured ways implied by their specialized approaches. That is perhaps the best sense in which a collection of essays could be said to be "interdisciplinary," and it is only to be hoped that the prodigious and suggestive world of Francophone hip-hop will receive, as a result of this collection, the kind of attention in the anglophone world that it surely merits.

WORKS CITED

Bazin, Hughes. *La Culture Hip Hop*. Paris: Desclee de Brouwer, 1995.

Krims, Adam. *Rap Music and the Poetics of Identity*. Cambridge: Cambridge UP, 2000.

La Haine. Dir. Mathieu Kassovitz. Les Productions Lazennec, 1995.

Milon, Alain. *L'Etranger dans la ville. Du rap au graff mural*. Paris: PUF, 1999.

Mitchell, Tony, ed. *Global Noise: Rap and Hip-Hop outside the USA*. Hanover, N.H.: Wesleyan UP, 2001.

Sayer, Derek. *The Violence of Abstraction: The Analytic Foundations of Historical Materialism*. Oxford: Blackwell, 1987.

Scott, Allen. *Metropolis: From the Division of Labor to Urban Form*. Berkeley: U of California P, 1988.

Acknowledgments

I appreciate the constant support and encouragement I received from my editors, Bruce Phillips, Rebecca Massa, Melissa Ray, and Kellie Hagan at Scarecrow Press. I thank them for having believed in this project from its earliest stage. I also want to extend my thanks to the many people who contributed their inspiration, advice, and support in the completion of this book: all the contributors and translators of this collection, for the quality of their work, patience, and capacity to work with sometimes tight deadlines, and the personnel of the University of Rhode Island's library—James Kinnie and Emily Greene, for their assistance in locating and ordering many books and documents useful to my research for this study, and the entire staff of the circulation desk.

Other people were very helpful in the completion of this project. At the University of Rhode Island, I thank in particular Melvin Wade at the Multicultural Center, who gave me the opportunity to start seriously thinking about this book; my colleagues Joseph Morello, David Gitlitz, and Kenneth Rogers, who shared their experiences and gave me great advice; and my students, whose enthusiastic comments and feedback contributed to the organization of this collection. I also owe a debt of gratitude to my friends Adam Krims, Allan Pasco, and Ralph Schoolcraft for their always very useful suggestions on various aspects of the work.

In addition, I want to acknowledge all the individuals who participated in the editing and design of the book: MC Solaar, Philippe Bordas, Virginie Vermonet, and Daniel Margules at DM Conseil; Assassin and Carine Chevanche at Delabel; Caroline Bonheur at Adam Production; François Poulain Massilia Sound System, Fabien Fragione,

IAM, SIYA PO'OSSI. X, Michelle Auzanneau, and Alain Milon. I would also like to thank L'Harmattan publishers for letting me reproduce a passage of chapter two, and Jean-Marie Jacono and Jacques Cheyronnaud for sharing all their contacts in France. Last but not least, thank you to my friend Didier Deroin and to his colleagues at tous des K, who generously offered to design the more than impressive cover of this book. Who would have thought back when we were classmates in high school in Aubagne, France, that Didier and I would collaborate on a book on hip-hop fifteen years later? Certainly not our professors. . . . I take this opportunity to thank all my friends who, back in high school in the 1980s, witnessed and embraced the birth of hip-hop with me. Wherever they are today, I send them my nostalgic greetings.

Finally and most importantly, I thank those people whose moral support keeps me going: my parents, my brother Eric, Sherri, my wife, and my two precious daughters, Chloé and Eva.

Introduction

Alain-Philippe Durand

This book is about the emergence and growing notoriety of rap music and hip-hop culture in France and the rest of the Francophone world. France has a long history of great admiration for African American musicians, and has often become a second home to black artists who were ignored or deemed undesirable in the United States. Josephine Baker, of course, is the most famous example, for she never had the career she deserved in America but was adored and celebrated by the French as one of the most respected performers in the history of the French Music Hall. Jazz is another musical style that has had a great influence on the French public ever since African American musicians toured the Paris scene, playing in improvised dance clubs in the cellars of Saint Germain in the 1950s. Throughout the years, performers such as Miles Davis, Dizzie Gillespie, and Billie Holiday, to name a few, attained superstar status in France. In a 1979 interview, Gillespie summarized the paradoxical situation of many African American musicians: "I found that strange, how blacks who had talent and couldn't get recognized in the United States would go over to Europe and immediately be appreciated and become big celebrities" (George, 201). It seems that no matter the style, the French will remain faithful to African American music. Indeed, jazz, blues, soul, and funk also found an immediate following in France. Singers and musicians like James Brown, Ray Charles, Aretha Franklin, Prince, and Tina Turner and groups like Kool and the Gang or Earth, Wind, and Fire still enjoy great success on the other side of the Atlantic. Given this constant attention and admiration for African American music, it's no surprise that the French would also embrace rap music and hip-hop culture in general. Since its arrival in the early 1980s, rap music in France has experienced an immediate and ever-growing success, going from an underground sound to becoming second only to rap music in the United States. The main reason for this rapid ascension is that if the French were originally seduced by American rappers such as Grandmaster Flash, the Sugar Hill Gang, or RUN DMC, they soon started to write and to record their own French language productions, creating at the same time a new form of rap. Furthermore, just as American rap crossed borders, French rap influenced artists in the rest of the Francophone world, especially western Africa and Quebec.

The purpose of this volume is to present and explain the success and importance of rap music in the Francophone world, and provide an introduction to the many forms of expression of French and Francophone hip-hop cultures. As Adam Krims points out (10–11), it is necessary to explain the use of the terms rap and hip-hop, which are often perceived in various ways by artists, fans, and scholars. This book follows Krims's definition of rap: a musical style belonging to hip-hop culture (Krims, 12). Hip-hop is understood in this collection as a culture that includes three main forms of expression: musical, verbal, and visual. These forms of expression are conveyed through rap music, hip-hop dance, and graffiti/tagging.

The title of this volume, *Black, Blanc, Beur*, is a play on the colors of the French flag: *bleu, blanc, rouge* (blue, white, red). This pun first appeared in the early 1990s in the north of France when it was used as the main slogan of an annual antiracist festival (Cannon, 154). It has been used since then on different occasions as a motto for ethnic diversity in France, the best example being the historic French victory in the World Cup soccer tournament in 1998. The French national team, which was composed of players representing various races and origins, caused such a strong unified celebration among the French people that the media revived the expression by referring to the country as "la France Black, Blanc, Beur" (Black, White, Beur France). The term *beur* was first used in Paris in the 1970s. It is a *verlan* (backslang) expression that "was formed by inverting the syllables of the word *Arabe*" (Hargreaves and McKinney, 20). *Beurs* are the children of immigrants from Algeria, Morocco, or Tunisia but are themselves born in France and are French citizens. According to journalist François Reynart, the French housing projects in the suburbs, the *banlieues*, reproduce the same multiethnic unification through hip-hop culture: "There is indeed a banlieue culture, rap, and verlan, but it belongs to all the inhabitants of the housing estate populated by as many whites as blacks and Beurs" (quoted in Rosello, 69).

Hip-hop culture has become such a social phenomenon in France that, since the early 1990s, it has regularly attracted the attention of the media and more recently the French academic community. The respected French national newspapers *Le Monde* and *Libération* regularly publish articles dealing with hip-hop, and *Libération* even produced a special issue dedicated to rap music in 1999. The first major scholarly contributions to French hip-hop appeared in the second half of the 1990s, and include the works of Hugues Bazin (1995), Olivier Cachin (1996), Anne-Marie Green (1997), Manuel Boucher (1998), Alain Milon (1999), and Médéric Gasquet-Cyrus (1999). In the English-speaking world, several important studies on rap music and hip-hop culture were published during the same period by authors such as Tricia Rose (1994), Russell Potter (1995), William Eric Perkins (1996), Nelson George (1998), and Adam Krims (2000). Yet, if some of these writers, like George and Krims, acknowledge and devote brief parts of their works to the expanding prevalence of hip-hop in France and in other countries, all these authors deal mainly with the phenomenon of rap and hip-hop in the United States. In fact, in the English-speaking world there does not yet exist a full-length study focusing on French and Francophone hip-hop.[1] Only a few publications, such as the ones written by Tony Mitchell (1996 and 2001), Andy Bennett (2000), and Alec Hargreaves and Mark McKinney (1997), include chapters on European rap music. In light of the increasing popularity of rap music and hip-hop culture in the Francophone world, this book intends to fill this gap.

Hip-hop culture affects so many parts of the French and Francophone societies that it was important for this study to use an interdisciplinary approach. It contains contributions by some of the most renowned hip-hop scholars on both sides of the Atlantic, and addresses hip-hop from the perspectives of various disciplines (anthropology, cultural studies, ethnology, history, linguistics, musicology, psychology, and sociology). André J. M. Prévos gives, in the first chapter, a history of French rap music from its origins to the present. Prévos not only introduces the groups from Paris and Marseilles—the two main poles of

French rap music—but he touches as well on lesser-known regions such as Brittany. In chapter two, Jean-Marie Jacono analyzes the musical techniques of the rap groups from Marseilles in order to establish a connection between this musical expression and the notion of identity. While Jacono concentrates on the music, Anthony Pecqueux pays close attention, in the third chapter, to the stage performances of the rap groups from Marseilles. In the following essay, Paul Silverstein concentrates on the Parisian rap act Suprême NTM and the national political debate this group provoked in 1995. In the fifth and sixth chapters, Manuel Boucher and Anne-Marie Green analyze the French public's perceptions of rap music. The two other forms of hip-hop expression are presented in chapters seven and eight. Alain Milon's contribution deals with the art of graffiti and tagging, while Hugues Bazin recounts the history of hip-hop dance in France. Finally, the last two chapters introduce different forms of rap music in two representative Francophone regions, Michelle Auzanneau concentrating on Gabon and Roger Chamberland focusing on Quebec.

NOTE

1. There are a few articles on French rap music that have been published in English in academic journals. See, for instance, André J. M. Prévos's contribution in *The French Review*.

WORKS CITED

Bazin, Hugues. *La Culture Hip-Hop*. Paris: Desclée de Brouwer, 1995.

Bennett, Andy. *Popular Music and Youth Culture: Music, Identity and Place*. London: Macmillan P, 2000.

Boucher, Manuel. *Rap, expression des lascars. Signification et enjeux du rap dans la société française*. Paris: L'Harmattan, 1998.

Cachin, Olivier. *L'offensive rap*. Paris: Découvertes/Gallimard, 1996.

Cannon, Steve. "Paname City Rapping: B-Boys in the Banlieues and Beyond."*Post-Colonial Cultures in France*. Eds. Alec G. Hargreaves and Mark McKinney. London: Routledge, 1997. 150–68.

Gasquet-Cyrus, Médéric, Guillaume Kosmicki, and Cécile Van der Avenne, eds. *Paroles et Musiques à Marseille*. Paris: L'Harmattan, 1999.

George, Nelson. *Hip-Hop America*. New York: Viking, 1998.

Green, Anne-Marie. *Des jeunes et des musiques. Rock, Rap, Techno*. Paris: L'Harmattan, 1997.

Hargreaves, Alec G., and Mark McKinney, eds. *Post-Colonial Cultures in France*. London: Routledge, 1997.

Krims, Adam. *Rap Music and the Poetics of Identity*. Cambridge: Cambridge UP, 2000.

Milon, Alain. *L'étranger dans la Ville. Du rap au graff mural*. Paris: PUF, 1999.

Mitchell, Tony. *Global Noise: Rap and Hip-Hop outside the USA*. Hanover,: Wesleyan UP, 2001.

———. *Popular Music and Local Identity. Rock, Pop and Rap in Europe and Oceania*. London: Leicester UP, 1996.

Perkins, William Eric. *Droppin' Science: Critical Essays on Rap Music and Hip Hop Culture*. Philadelphia: Temple University Press, 1996.

Potter, Russell. *Spectacular Vernaculars: Hip-Hop and the Politics of Post-modernism*. Albany: SUNY P, 1995.

Prévos, André J. M. "The Evolution of French Rap Music and Hip-Hop Culture in the 1980s and 1990s." *The French Review* 69.5 (1996): 713–25.

Rose, Tricia. *Black Noise: Rap Music and Black Culture in Contemporary America*. Hanover: Wesleyan UP, 1994.

Rosello, Mireille. *Declining the Stereotype: Ethnicity and Representation in French Culture*. Hanover: UP of New England, 1998.

1

Two Decades of Rap in France: Emergence, Developments, Prospects

André J. M. Prévos

FROM PARIS TO NEW YORK CITY AND BACK

In France as well as in Great Britain, the second half of the 1970s was marked by a strong anti-disco movement that led to the emergence of punk in Great Britain and to the so-called *alternative movement* in France. In France, *alternative music* emerged in the early 1980s, notably with groups such as Bérurier Noir and Les Garçons Bouchers when the first rap tunes from the United States appeared (Prévos, 1991). Among the strongest supporters of the anti-disco movement in France were young immigrants from the Caribbean residing in France. These youngsters gathered in clubs and dance halls where the music they liked was played constantly by disc jockeys. One of these clubs, named *L'Émeraude* (The Emerald) had a disc jockey named Sidney. He played salsa, reggae, and African popular music to his customers who prided themselves in attending the only disco in Paris where disco music was never heard (Bocquet and Pierre-Adolphe, 14).

In 1981, François Mitterrand was elected President of the French Republic and his election had a significant impact upon the national organization of radio broadcasting in France. Until 1981, the French government was the only legal entity that had the right to broadcast radio inside France. A consequence was that all the radios that were not part of the French radio system had their broadcasting towers beyond the French borders. In 1981, after the law was changed and so-called "free radios" were allowed to broadcast on the FM band, such radios emerged in Paris. One of them was Carbone 14 in the fourteenth *arrondissement*

of the city. The station started broadcasting twenty-four hours per day
on 14 December 1981. Two of its most popular disc jockeys were Phil
Barney and Dee Nasty. In addition to being a disc jockey for Carbone
14, Barney worked for a company that imported American records for
the disc jockeys of Parisian *discothèques*. Barney started imitating
American disc jockeys who used to talk during the musical introduction
of the record they were playing. In his own way, Barney may be seen as
the creator of a technique that would be developed by rappers. Dee
Nasty was familiar with African American rap because he had contacts
in the United States who had told him how to develop his "spinning"
skills by replacing the rubber plate of the vinyl record player with a hard
plastic plate so that he could accelerate the spinning speed of the record
to reach more rapidly the excerpt he wanted to play. Dee Nasty was thus
recreating techniques used by early Jamaican disc jockeys such as Kool
Herc (Rockwell, 2:23).

In the early 1980s, two Frenchmen in New York City played a noticeable role in the history of early American rap. Bernard Zekri had left
France in 1980 and worked in a French restaurant in New York City. In
addition, he was a fixture in the Thirteenth Avenue clubs where b-boys
from the Bronx used to gather. At the end of 1980, Jean Karakos, who
had been at the head of Celluloid, a small French record label, arrived
in New York City and met Zekri. The latter was a good friend of Afrika
Bambaata and it was rumored that Zekri was the only white person who
could walk the streets of the Bronx at any time of day or night without
any fear of ever being mistreated. In France, Karakos had published
records by The Toasters and The Last Poets; the emergence of rap did
not surprise him at all (Bocquet and Pierre-Adolphe, 30). Karakos and
Zekri have left a trace in the early history of rap in New York City. First,
with Tom Silverman of the Tommy Boy label, they were the co-creators
of the twelve-inch 45–rpm record that emerged as the early vinyl rap
record format of choice in New York City (between 1980 and 1985). In
addition, in 1982, Karakos and Zekri organized the *New York City Rap
Tour* in Europe that played in France between 21 and 28 November
1982. For many French youngsters this was the first time they had the
chance to see and hear African American rappers (Beckman and Adler,
17). Shortly before the tour, Zekri and Karakos had recorded Fab 5
Freddy and were left with an empty side on the record. They asked
Zekri's girlfriend to record a rap in French; "Change de Beat" by B-Side
was recorded in 1982 in New York City but its impact in France was

hardly noticeable because the record was not made available through the usual distribution channels in that country.

The French press was taking note of the presence of rappers in New York City. In October 1982, the French newspaper *Libération* published a series of daily reports about the so-called street culture of New York City and its boroughs (Thibodat, 21). It was also at that same time that the French group Chagrin d'Amour recorded its eponymous album whose songs did not pretend to be rap but whose performance techniques had evidently been borrowed from those of American rappers (Chagrin d'Amour; Laville, 128).

FROM THE BRONX TO THE FRENCH *BANLIEUE*

In 1984, Africa Bambaataa came to France and established a French branch of his movement—the Zulu Nation. Unfortunately, the results were rather disappointing and were not at all commensurate with Bambaataa's efforts. When the Zulus tried to establish themselves in the French *banlieues*—essentially around Paris—their coming was not widely accepted because the popularity of hip-hop in France was ebbing at the time. Furthermore, several components of the teachings of the Zulu Nation were not at all popular among the French *banlieue* youth. First, the Zulus were opposed to graffiti that were emerging in France around that time. Also, young robbers who stole the purses and billfolds of subway passengers were often dressed in the Zulu style. The victims clearly identified these clothing details as specific characteristics of the young gangsters who ransacked the subway lines in the French capital. For the French press, the term Zulu became a synonym for "young gang member from the popular suburbs" (Louis and Prinaz, 170–96). By the mid-1990s in the French *banlieues* the Zulu Nation had lost most of its impact as well as most of its members.

The 1990s have been marked by a large number of studies of the young people who live in these popular suburban areas of French cities. David Lepoutre has underlined three major characteristics of these youth groups in the French *banlieue*. First, the members of these groups have several types of organization; sometimes they are organized according to rules encountered in American gangs, at other times they resemble more a grouping of young members of the same age living in a place that they "mark" as their own. Once they have established their control over this area, they create their own forms of social interaction. Members of such groups recognize each other through their language, a slang that incorporates elements from the French *verlan*, words from the speech patterns of the languages of their parents (Arabic, African dialects, etc.) and a large number of insults and other obscene words. Many French *banlieue* youths may thus be said to share several points with their young American counterparts from African American ghettos: their "appropriation" of the space where they evolve, their own "slang" and similar attitudes towards music, rap, and break dancing, as well as a shared focus on their "honor" (Lepoutre, 34–112).

   The history of graffiti in France, however, allows for a differentiation of the evolution between France and the United States. In his study, Alain Vulbeau underlines the fact that the French press took note of the American graffiti only in 1981, seldom mentioned them before 1986, and showed an interest in French tag artists only in 1989. In the 1990s, the multiplication of tags in France and the efforts of the French police led to the condemnation of tag artists who had to clean up their tags and, at times, to pay a fine in addition. Between 1988 and 1995, the attitude towards tag artists changed, it evolved from tolerance to restriction (Vulbeau, 35–49).

THE EMERGENCE OF RAP IN THE FRENCH *BANLIEUE*

The youth culture of the French *banlieue* gained a foothold throughout the country in the 1980s and 1990s. It was during these years that French youth became aware of African American hip-hop culture and that they adapted it to their own situation. The first type of hip-hop manifestation to emerge in France in the 1980s was break dancing (breaking or locking in the United States). The first television program devoted to hip-hop in France was a program named *Hip-Hop* entirely devoted to break dancing; the show was presented by Sidney on the TF1 television channel in 1984 and 1985 (Peigne-Giuly, 34). The program ended abruptly in 1985 and led to a clear reorientation of most youngsters from the French *banlieues* from break dancing to rapping (Cachin and Dupuis, 15). The first rap recordings in French were produced in 1985. In 1984, Dee Nasty recorded his *Paname City Rapping*, an independently produced album that was sold in the streets because no commercial French record label wanted to produce and distribute an album by a French rapper. These early rap tunes in French were recorded at a time when French rappers were still closely following the techniques developed by their African American models. A few French rappers tried to record raps in English but they soon switched to French because they were aware that they did not sound as good as those African American models. Lionel D. is the only rapper in France who has insisted upon the fact that, when he was going to perform raps in French on Sidney's program on Radio 7, he was one of a small group of rappers who performed in French (Cachin, 68).

In 1990, the publication of the French anthology *Rapattitudes* was seen as the consecration of rap in France. This album was produced by a large recording company and featured the works of ten artists and groups of French rappers. The large popular success of this first anthology encouraged French record companies to sign rap performers. In 1990, Lionel D.'s album *Y'a pas de problème* was published but did not sell very well. Some argued that the sudden publication of two rap albums in a short period of time had caused a "glut" of rap records—even though it is hard to imagine a "glut" of two albums. It has also been said that the album was of average quality and that the serious lyrics of all the songs may have caused its lack of popularity. Finally, Lionel D. has been accused of not having supported the publication of his album in an acceptable manner. Lionel D. has repeated that he always refused to dress up as a b-boy and that he had to cancel several concerts because he was too drunk to step on the stage. His label voided his recording contract; today Lionel D. is known only by those who are familiar with the early years of rap in France. In 1992, a second volume of *Rapattitudes* was published but had less impact than the first volume because more rap artists had been recorded and had become well situated at the top of the French popular charts.

A quick look at the early rap groups and rap artists in France makes it clear that it is impossible to indicate a clear-cut "ethnic integrity" among these artists. In the United States, the great majority of rappers are African American (there have been few exceptions such as the Beastie Boys or Eminem) while in France they are of varied ethnic origins, from North Africa to Black Africa, and from the Caribbean to the French *banlieue*. For example, the artists featured on the *Rapattitude* anthology included Dee Nasty, a white artist from the Parisian *banlieue*; EJM had parents from Martinique and Cameroon. Lionel D.'s parents are black and white; Les Little MC

are blacks from Africa and the Caribbean; Saliha's parents are Arab
and Italian. The members of Suprême NTM are white and Caribbean;
Jhonnygo was a young black African, while the group Nec Plus Ul-
tra was composed of young white Frenchmen from the nineteenth *arrondissement* of Paris (Cannon, p. 154). The ethnic diversity of rappers in France is now a widely recognized fact (Leland, Mabry, and
Thomas, 42–43).

RAP IN FRANCE IN THE 1990S

MC Solaar: An African Dandy Who Raps

In 1990, MC Solaar recorded his first twelve-inch 45–rpm record with the
title "Bouge de là" (Move Away from There); the record sold very well and
Solaar was soon invited to perform with well-known French pop groups
such as Niagara (Puma, 23). In 1991, Solaar's first album *Qui sème le vent
récolte le tempo* (He Who Sows Wind, Shall Harvest Tempo) established
him in a high position both with rap fans as well as with older music fans
who enjoyed the underlying humor as well as the highly poetic features of
his lyrics. Soon, Solaar became a fixture on French television: he underlined his familiarity with French poets as well as his efforts geared towards
the composition of intelligent lyrics with a faultless musical accompaniment (Davet, 1997: 24). Solaar's popularity lasted throughout the 1990s.

Solaar is seen as the middle between two extreme positions. The first
position is defended by those who see rap in France as a production
whose lyrics fall well within the French poetic tradition and whose musical accompaniment contributes to its overall quality. Those who defend this position see Solaar as the perfect example of what a rapper
should be. The second position is defended by those who accuse Solaar
of having abandoned rap's basic ideology in order to become a show-
business star. For those who hold this position, the defense of a *banlieue*
ideal is essential. Solaar sees himself well within this overall position
when he claims that his most notable contribution has been the erasure
of clichés associated with the *banlieue* (Barbot, 76–81). Solaar has also
participated in the expansion of rap by founding his own label *Sentinel
Nord* in 1995 and by recording groups such as Démocrates D and Les
Sages Poètes de la Rue. By the end of the 1990s, with six albums under
his belt, Solaar had reached a high level of popular recognition as was

illustrated by his selection as a member of the jury of the 1998 Cannes Film Festival (Touraine and Marizy, 104), and his discussion with French writer Maurice Druon (Delétraz).

Benny B and Les Inconnus

In 1990–1991, Benny B became a popular rapper in France because of the attractiveness of his stage persona and because of the fact that he positioned himself as a precursor of rap in France. In their recordings, Benny B and the members of his group described themselves as the originators of rap in France and underlined their hopes to popularize this new musical form as a solution to the problems facing young Frenchmen from financially disadvantaged groups. They also made it clear that they did not want to associate with any politician and that their only goal was to place rap in France at a high level that would help French b-boys. Benny B and his DJ—Daddy K—have often been accused of presenting an image close to that presented by American rapper Vanilla Ice (Handelman, 34). The group saw itself as "clean" and as rappers of a high level. Such clear-cut self-aggrandizement contributed significantly to the rapid loss of popularity of the group. Their second album sold poorly and the group had disappeared from the French charts by the mid-1990s.

In 1991, the French group Les Inconnus (The Unknowns) recorded a 45–rpm single with two titles exploiting the new popularity of rap. Les Inconnus is a French group famous for its humorous sketches. On this record, they offered two images of rap; the first "Auteuil, Neuilly, Passy (*banlieue* sud)" presents a very bourgeois image of rap. It is known that, in the early 1980s, young bourgeois from Paris traveled to New York City and brought back rap records that were the "up-to-date thing" to listen to. The second "C'est ton destin (*banlieue* nord)" is more realistic but not necessarily closer to reality. This record was very popular in France because its excesses paralleled those of some rappers in France, without the underlying violence often associated with rappers.

Zulu Rappers in France

Two French groups have been associated with Bambaataa's ideals: Les Little and Sens Unik. *Les Vrais* (The Real Ones), the first album by Les Little was published in 1992. The lyrics underline the philosophy of the Zulu Nation. In "Les Vrais" (The Real Ones), they introduce themselves and emphasize the fact that their clothes look more "disco" than "hip-hop." In "Une journée de fous" (A Crazy Day), they criticize the attitudes of the French police as well as the dangerous environment of the French *banlieue*. Les Little do not openly declare themselves associated with Bambaataa but their overall attitude and their lyrics make evident their following of Bambaataa's teachings.

The four albums by Sens Unik, whose members come from Lausanne, Switzerland, also make it clear that the group is close to Bambaataa's ideals. In their second album (*Sens Unik*), two tunes make this evident. The first, "Tue ton poste" (Kill Your TV), focuses on the danger of television transforming its listeners and poisoning their lives. In "La horde des faux" (The Hord of Fakes), they introduce their listeners to those fakes for whom they have only contempt.

The group Assassin was close to the Zulu Nation and clearly situated within the hardcore stylistic realm. In "Respecte l'ancienne école" (Respect the Old School), they see themselves as members of the French hip-hop tradition and refuse to be told what to do or how to do it. In "Au centre des polémiques" (At the Core of Polemics), they make fun of French record companies who missed out entirely on the French rap wave of the mid-1980s, and in "A qui l'histoire?" (To Whom History?), they criticize the French school system for its lack of denunciation of the French colonizers of the nineteenth century. Assassin is one of the rare French rap groups that has recorded about the environment; in "L'écologie: Sauvons la planète" (Ecology: Let's Save the Planet), they denounce the destruction of natural environments through administrative or governmental decisions (Assassin).

Solo is an artist close to the Zulu philosophy whose role has been essentially in the background of the rap scene in France. In 1984, Bambaataa chose him as a "Zulu King." He has worked with several groups on significant projects but he does admit that today the Zulu Nation does not exist any more in France (Keita, 22).

Hardcore Rappers in France

The hardcore movement is not characterized by any specific philosophical basis but by its fast rhythm (in beats per minute) and its "cruder" musical accompaniment; in addition, hardcore lyrics tend to be harsher than those of other styles. Several French groups have been identified as typical exponents of the style; among the latter are Assassin,

Suprême NTM, and Ministère AMER. These groups do not see them-selves as French representatives of the Californian "gangsta rap." They consider their mission to be the denunciation of what they see as the so-cial and economic exploitation of marginal groups and individuals in French society (Bocquet and Pierre-Adolphe, 52, 100).

Suprême NTM is seen as the most representative group of the hardcore movement in France. Kool Shen (Bruno Lopes) and Joey Starr (Didier Morville), the two members of the group, have been part of the French hip-hop movement since 1983. They started as break-dancers and graffiti artists but moved to rapping when they no-ticed the impact of the rappers. They claim that they selected their name, which is understood as the abbreviation of "Nique ta mère" (F**k Your Mother), after one of their friends, who was employed by an ad agency, was asked to elaborate a poster project for a customer who did not want to have his real name used until he accepted the overall design of the poster. Lopes and Morville claim that their friend had written *Nick Thamaire* in the space where the name of the customer would be featured and that they decided to use this name as their stage name in 1987 (Bocquet and Pierre-Adolphe, 100). Be-tweeen 1987 and 1990, they participated in several *Paris Cup of the DJs* and, in 1990, they recorded their "Je rap" (I Rap) for the *Rapat-titude* anthology (Rapattitude).

Authentik, their first album, was published in 1991 and sold very well. The lyrics in this album underlined the claim of the title: the true association between the members of the group and the *banlieue* lifestyle. In the song "De personne je ne serai la cible" (I'll Be No-body's Target), they introduced themselves as "NTM, indivisible, in-corrigible, incorruptible." In 1993, their second album *1993 . . . j'ap-puie sur la gâchette* (1993 . . . I Squeeze the Trigger) was sometimes seen as an attempt to associate themselves with the California gangsta rap movement since there was a .45 colt on the album's cover. NTM answered that the handgun was featured on the album cover because it was associated with the tune of that same title in which the hero commits suicide with a .45 handgun. In "La révolu-tion du son" (The Revolution of Sound), they underlined the fact that rap was a force—a revolution?—that had invaded the popular music scene in France and that those in power tried to silence. In their song "Police," they characterized the police as "a brainless machine under Justice's orders and upon which I pee." Those who saw the group's

1997 condemnation for "violence against the forces of law and order" as an attempt to censure their lyrics have often quoted these words. However, as I have shown, their words were not said during the song but between songs and thus lost their "artistic creation" coverage and fell under the antiracism law of France (Prévos, 1998: 67–84). In 1995, their third album *Paris sous les bombes* (Paris under the Bombs) refers to the aerosol spray cans (*bombes* in French) used by graffiti artists and not to explosive devices. In this album, they denounce the National Front, France's neo-Nazi political organization, and express their hope to see France's societal order reshaped. Today, each member of the group has founded his own record label and it seems that the recording career of Suprême NTM has been put on hold.

All the members of Ministère AMER came from the *banlieue* city of Sarcelles and considered themselves part of the hardcore movement in France. Their album *Pourquoi tant de haine?* (Why So Much Hate?) was published in 1992 and had much success, essentially because of the tune "Brigitte (femme de flic)" (Brigitte [Cop's Wife]). Several police unions launched complaints against the tune but they could not make them stick for two reasons: first, they launched their complaints more than six months after the publication of the tune and, second, because the lyrics fell under the French law protecting "artistic creations." In their second album, the group recorded a new version of "Brigitte" but also recorded "Nègres de la pègre" (Blacks from the Underworld) that underlined the fact that many blacks in France are associated with criminal groups. After having been dragged before judges for "appeal to hate and crime," each of the members decided to go for a solo career (Puma, 32).

The popularity of hardcore groups in France is influenced by several factors. First, the violence of the lyrics may be seen as an equivalent of the "explicit lyrics" stickers used in the United States after Tipper Gore and the PMRC launched their censorship campaign against rap in the late 1980s. Second, the fact that they seldom appeared on television often forced their listeners to buy their albums in order to (re)discover the lyrics. Finally, the harsh accusations against the French police as well as the denunciations of the French justice system were based on well-documented cases of excesses; this contributed significantly to the credibility of the sometimes outlandish accusations voiced by hardcore rappers in France.

Other "Ideological" Rappers in France

The rappers who emerged in France in the 1980s came mostly from the Parisian *banlieues*. However, the *banlieues* of many large cities in France were also marked by the emergence of rap. Such was the case of Marseilles, famous in France for being the birthplace of the group IAM. The members of the group assembled between 1985 and 1989, first under the stage name B-Boy Stance and, later, under the name IAM. They also chose to perform in French. Their career was launched in 1990 when they participated in Madonna's *Blonde Ambition Tour*. Each member of the group has a stage persona based on the names of famous Egyptian pharaohs. Their choice of Egypt (instead of Algeria) as a representation of the Arab world was a wise one because Egypt is mentioned in all French textbooks for its impact on early Western civilizations while Algeria is mentioned in the news mainly for the many assassinations by Arab fundamentalists. The members of IAM also got a firsthand knowledge of American rap during their trips to the United States in the second half of the 1980s (Deroin, Guilledoux, Muntaner, and Rof, 10–23).

I have called pharaohism the ideological foundation of IAM's albums because the group's philosophy focuses on the importance of the pharaohs and their possible role in today's world (Prévos, 1996: 720–21). In addition to their ideological compositions, the members of IAM also deal with their city's society and problems: the influence of the National Front, drug trafficking, criminal activities, etc. Moreover, IAM's compositions also include a fair amount of humor. Such is the case with "La méthode Marsimil" (The Marsimil Method), which narrates the adventures of a young American who came to Marseilles to learn French with the members of IAM who, after several months with the group, could only use insults and popular expressions picked up during soccer games.

THE "SECOND GENERATION" OF RAPPERS IN FRANCE

By the mid-1990s, rappers in France had established their stylistic repertoires. We have seen that the groups sharing the hardcore beliefs form the most significant block of rappers in France. Nevertheless, the impact of more specific artists cannot be denied. The impact of MC Solaar has been significant throughout the 1990s, as has been that of IAM; two artists whose ideologies differ but whose impact on the development of rap in France has been significant. It was at this time that emerged what has come to be called the "second generation of rappers in France." Several trends were clearly noticeable in this new group of artists who, having seen the emergence of rap, elaborated their own stylistic references in an effort to gain recognition by enthusiasts of popular music.

Alliance Ethnik and "Popular Rap"

As its name suggests, Alliance Ethnik is a symbolic association of its members, all from different ethnic backgrounds. Several of them participated in the sessions leading to *Rapattitudes*; Fast J, the group's DJ, was among those who helped with the recordings by Saliha and New Generation. In 1995, their first album, *Simple et Funky*, was a significant success and became a platinum seller (one million copies sold) in 1996. The lyrics of the group's tunes underlined their positive approach towards life as well as their focus on life's most pleasurable moments. Several groups tried to imitate Alliance Ethnik but their attempts were fruitless because they could not duplicate the spinning techniques of the group's DJs K-Mel and Crazy B. The group's second album in 1999 was much less successful and the future of the group remains unclear. Among the groups that have recorded similar albums are Reciprok whose album *Il y a des jours comme ça* (There Are Days Like That) was characterized by lyrics without much ideological impact and by a strong focus on relations between the sexes. The career of Ménélik, a member of MC Solaar's posse, is more particular since he was discovered in Spain and in Japan before he recorded his first album in France. His two albums, *Phénoménélik* and *Je me souviens* (I Remember), were well received during the second half of the 1990s. Mellowman and KDD (a group from the Toulouse *banlieue*) are two groups that belong to the Alliance Ethnik stylistic family.

Ragamuffin Artists in France

Tonton David (Uncle David) was one of the first and the most popular of the ragamuffin artists in France. His tune "Peuples du monde" (People of the World) was one of the most popular tunes in the *Rapattitudes* anthology and is said to have been a major factor in the popular success of this album. His two albums *Le blues des racailles* (The Scummer's

Blues) and *Allez leur dire* (Go Tell Them) were also very successful. His followers accused him of "treason" during the second half of the 1990s because he tried to diversify his musical productions and used musicians instead of DJs; his career suffered significantly and is at a low level today. Two groups from French Provence have also had a noticeable impact on the world of ragamuffin in France. Pouppa Claudio from Toulon recorded two albums in 1991 and 1994 (Beaucourt, 21) and Massilia Sound System from Marseilles, still active today, participated in the emergence of their city as a center for ragamuffin and rap. The members of Massilia Sound System helped those of IAM when the latter started their musical career. Throughout the 1990s, both groups have emphasized their regional attachment and their desire to see Marseilles recognized as an important cultural center in France (Deroin, Guilledoux, Muntaner, and Rof, 6–11).

In 1992, the group Saï Saï recorded its first album and was featured in the French press when, in 1995, they performed in Sarajevo. Daddy Yod began his career in the French Caribbean but, in spite of a good album in 1997, his career appears to be in decline. As for the lyrics of the group Raggasonic, they are closer to reggae and hardcore rap. The members of Neg' Marrons are very close to those of Ministère AMER as is illustrated by their album *Rue Case Nègres*, inspired by the title of Joseph Zobel's novel (Zobel).

Fabe is an artist of the "second generation" whose impact during the second half of the 1990s has been significant. He has recorded three albums of high quality: *Béfa surprend ses frères* (Béfa—the verlan of Fabe—Surprises his Brothers), *Le fond et la forme* (The Idea and the Style) and *Détournement de son* (Highjacking of Sound) in 1998. Soon E MC and Démocrates D are two groups associated with MC Solaar's posse—the so-called "500 one posse"—but their recordings clearly indicate that they are not imitators of MC Solaar. Démocrates D has been seen as a group defending the ideals of the Nation of Islam because they always wear dark suits, white shirts and neckties and dark sunglasses. Les sages poètes de la rue (The Wise Poets from the Street) are also associated with MC Solaar but cannot be seen as imitators either.

Women Rap Artists in France

Saliha has been considered as the first female rap artist in France; she recorded a tune on the *Rapattitude* anthology of 1990. She recorded two albums in the first half of the 1990s. The first, *Unique* in 1992, had limited impact while her second was better received, essentially because of the tune "16 ans neuf mois et un bébé sur les bras" (16 Years and Nine Months Old with a Baby to Take Care Of). Unfortunately, Saliha has not recorded since 1994 (Saliha). B-Love recorded her tune "Lucy" on *Rap-attitudes 2* in 1992 and her first album, *B Love,* appeared in 1996. Mélaaz has been associated with MC Solaar since his early successes; she participated in the recording of "Bouge de là" as well as in the recording of several others of Solaar's tunes. Her album *Mélaaz* recorded in 1995 sold rather poorly (Mélaaz). New artists appeared during the second half of the 1990s and have left their mark in the development of rap in France. Sté Strausz offers an exemplary illustration, she recorded several tunes for anthologies before she produced her first album and has acquired a wide reputation because of her noticeable use of slang (Night, 26). The end of the 1990s marked a clear evolution in the feminine rap productions in France. Many popular weekly magazines—such as *L'Express*—noticed this fact and mentioned it in their pages. The author of the essay in *L'Express* underlined the fact that most new feminine rap artists in France were from Africa and analyzed this new situation as the realization of what he called a "black manifesto." French women rap artists share attitudes similar to those of their male counterparts: they strongly oppose the National Front; they chronicle the life of the *banlieue* from a new point of view (a feminine point of view); they share a critical view of the media; and they underline the fact they should be judged as artists and not as women (Dupont, 112–13).

The End of the 1990s

The authors of *Rap ta France* have underlined the fact that the years 1995–1996 were marked by a sharp increase in the number of rap albums produced in France. By their own estimation, they indicate that one album was produced in 1984, three in 1988, three in 1990, eight in 1991, nine in 1992, eight in 1993, nine in 1994, twenty-three in 1995, fifty-three in 1996, and fifteen between 1 January and 28 February 1997 (Bocquet and Pierre-Adolphe, 251–63). During these years, the major rappers in France continued to record; IAM, MC Solaar, and Suprême NTM published albums that sold very well.

A few artists of note have emerged during the late 1990s. Yazid was noted for his first album *Je suis l'Arabe* (I Am the Arab) while the

group Expression Direkt got much closer to the hardcore stylistic domain that the earlier recordings had suggested. The group Les Gens
(The People) was noted for the significant amount of Anglo-American
expressions in its lyrics. The music of Légitime Processus is a mixture
of rap and reggae with soul and funk, while the group LAMIFA focuses on "controlling the street" and everything that happens there as
their two albums suggest (LAMIFA, 1996 and 1998). The group
2'Bal'2Neg, which was dissolved at the end of 1997, was frankly a
hardcore group, while the group Tout Simplement Noir (Simply
Black) had a more diversified repertory, mixing amusing or serious
lyrics and updating old traditional French songs (Tout Simplement
Noir). As for Doc Gynéco, his "sexy" lyrics (Doc Gynéco, 1996 and
1998) brought him fame before he became one of the major poles of
Secteur Ä (Fraisse, 16–17). The end of the 1990s saw as well the
emergence of Oxmo Puccino whose operatic treatment of the everyday life of the *banlieue* (Oxmo Puccino) was noted (Formula 2A2H,
22–24; Pliskin, 27). Driver has been associated with the hardcore underground movement but none of these elements is found in his album
nor in his image—that of a black golfer (Keita, 15). For Idéal J and
CMP Familia, the hardcore ties are unmistakable.

TOWARD A "REGIONALIZATION" OF RAP IN FRANCE?

I have already underlined the fact that the members of IAM have always emphasized that they are from Marseilles. It has also been made
clear that many groups from the Parisian *banlieue* have participated
in the "representation" of the latter. The huge success of Manau in
1998–1999 (their first album reached the platinum level), a group
composed of young men born in the Parisian *banlieue* of parents
from Brittany, once associated with the success of the Occitan group
Fabulous Trobadors, or KDD, both from Toulouse, along with
NAP—standing for New African Poets—from Strasbourg (Jehli 52),
led some observers to believe in the emergence of a "regional rap"
movement similar to the regional folk movements of the 1960s. It
may be much better to follow Nelson George who, in his characterization of American rap, has indicated that there was a "regionaliza-
tion of rap" instead of the emergence of a "regional rap." This remark, based on the development of the Atlanta and New Orleans

styles (Jermaine Dupri, Master P), does indeed illustrate what has happened in France in the late 1990s (George, 131–32).

RAP AND BUSINESS IN FRANCE

Many American rap magazines feature ads with rap artists. In France, this trend has not yet been noted. One reason may be that most of the French rappers are often strongly opposed to business ideals and often see record companies as the "enemy." However, the second half of the 1990s has been marked in France by the realization of the impact of rap artists on the part of the French business establishment. This was illustrated in 1996 when the French business magazine *Le Nouvel Econo-miste* selected the members of the group IAM as "men of the year" (A, C., iv). The group is at the head of several enterprises related to stage setting, show production, and recording that allow them to operate as a semi-independent entity associated with their record company. The group has produced recordings by other artists from Marseilles as well as its own albums according to its own schedule. Several other artists and groups have created their own labels. I have mentioned earlier that in 1995, MC Solaar created his own label *Sentinel Nord*, which has published albums by artists from the Parisian *banlieue*s. Each of the members of Suprême NTM has his own label as well. Kool Shen is in charge of *IV My People*, a label that records artists well within the boundaries of the hardcore style and usually publishes anthologies instead of albums by a single artist (IV My People). Joey Starr heads the label *BOSS* (for Boss of Scandalz Strategyz) that also published anthologies of artists in the hardcore stylistic domain (BOSS). Both artists, as well as some of their friends, sometimes participate in the recordings of these new performers.

Another type of artistic association is the one known under the name *Secteur Ä*. This group of performers is composed of artists all from Sarcelles, a *banlieue* of the French capital. They each have their own recording contracts with their specific record companies. However, when they record together, they do it under the name *Secteur Ä*, as an entity separate from the artistic entity represented by each of the artists belonging to this association. This was the case when the artists from *Secteur Ä* recorded together at the Parisian music hall Olympia and produced a double album documenting the show (Davet, 1998: 8–9).

CONCLUDING REMARKS

The impact of rap in France in the 1990s has been significant among French youth, whether from the *banlieues* or from less disadvantaged sociocultural environments. Many French youngsters, who are sharp observers of the influence from the United States when it comes to fashion or new musical developments, listen attentively to the music. The impact of rap in France is also noticeable from a purely financial standpoint. The records produced by the record companies sell in large numbers and contribute to the overall financial well being of these companies. It has already been suggested that the impact of rap in France is significant. In spite of the drop in overall record sales in 1999—whether due to larger use of MP3 downloading or due to illegal reproduction of albums with a computer by downloading the data of the album and engraving new copies with a CD-ROM engraver (Mortaigne, 1)—sales of rap recordings do represent a noticeable part of overall record sales in France.

Several types of evolution, based on what has happened in the United States, may be suggested for rap in France. A first possibility is the continuation of the significant financial impact of rap record sales in the overall income of record companies and a possible growth in the sociocultural impact of rap artists throughout the French sociocultural environment. It is doubtful that there will be many French rap artists in the world of advertising as is the case with African American rap artists in advertisements for so-called "street fashion" (Phat Farm, FUBU, etc.) in magazines such as *The Source* or *Vibe*. The major reason for this remark is that in France rap artists do not see themselves as part of the fashion world. Moreover, they may fear a backlash from their musical followers if they take part in an advertising campaign. It should be added that, with the exception of movie stars, few French popular artists appear in advertising campaigns in France. A second possibility could be the passage of rap artists to the world of cinema as has been the case in the United States with Ice T and Ice Cube in particular. Such a possibility may exist but, once again, the rappers may wish to choose carefully the type of character they would play in a movie. For example, it would be impossible to imagine the members of the group Suprême NTM—condemned for abusing women in airplanes and in their personal relations—playing romantic characters on the big screen (A., C., 11; "Joey Starr," 1). Moreover, there is not yet in France a tradition of *banlieue* cinema as there is in the United States with so-called "ghetto movies" or blaxploitation movies. To be sure, there was Matthieu Kassovitz's motion picture *La Haine* (Hate) in 1994 that was filmed in the *banlieue* and described the life in this environment. A third possibility could be a loss of impact of rap because of a long presence in the charts and of a loss of interest on the part of listeners as well as record buyers. This evolution of popular movements is well known. These popular movements become "old," lose their attractiveness and vanish from their dominant position before a new movement replaces them. This possibility is not likely given the present-day situation of rap in France as well as the situation of its American counterpart in the United States. The fact that rap is encountered in many countries, whether in Europe, in the Far East, or in Africa may be seen as a generalization of the impact of this African American music and its grounding in the history of world popular music. Whether rap will remain at such a level of popularity is truly hard to gauge and, for the time being, no reliable explanatory model has been advanced for a justification of its possible loss of importance among French youngsters.[1]

NOTE

1. Support for the writing of this essay came from a sabbatical leave during the 1998–1999 academic year and from a Research Development Grant (Summer 2000) from the Pennsylvania State University's Associate Dean for Faculty and Research of the Commonwealth College. In addition, I acknowledge the help from my colleague, Pr. Philip Mosley, in the proofreading of the final draft of this essay. However, any remaining stylistic shortcomings are my own.

WORKS CITED

A., C. "NTM cogne les filles." *Mariane* 7–13 Dec. 1998: 11.
Barbot, Philippe. "MC Solaar. Palabres exquis." *Télérama* 28 May 1997: 76–81.
Beaucourt, Daniel. "Pouppa Claudio: Ragamuffin avec l'accent." *Télé-Poche* 18–24 Jul. 1992: 21.
Beckman, Jeannette, and B. Adler. *Rap: Portraits and Lyrics of a Generation of Black Rockers.* London: Omnibus Press, 1991.
Bocquet, José-Louis, and Philippe Pierre-Adolphe. *Rap ta France.* Paris: Flammarion, 1997.

C., A. "Marseille 1996: Hommes de l'année." *Le Nouvel Économiste* 9 Feb. 1996: iv.

Cachin, Olivier. *L'offensive rap*. Paris: Découvertes/Gallimard, 1996.

Cachin, Olivier, and Jérôme Dupuis. "Le rap sort de la zone rouge." *Le Nouvel Observateur* 9–15 Aug. 1990: 15.

Cannon, Steve. "Paname City Rapping. B-boys in the *Banlieues* and Beyond." In *Post-Colonial Cultures in France*. Eds. Alec C. Hargreaves and Mark McKinney. London: Routledge, 1997. 150–65.

Davet, Stéphane. "Les soldats-businessmen du rap." *Le Monde* 5 Mar. 1998: 8–9.

———. "MC Solaar, héritier rappeur du dandysme à la française." *Le Monde* 11 Jun. 1997: 24.

Delétraz, François. "Druon: feu vert pour le rap. Maurice Druon-MC Solaar. Au menu, un sujet qui leur tient à coeur, les mots." *Le Figaro Littéraire* 31 Jan. 1998: 82–85.

Deroin, Didier, Fred Guilledoux, Stéphan Muntaner, and Gilles Rof. *IAM. Le livre*. Toulon: Soleil Productions—Plein Sud, 1996.

Dupont, Pascal. "Les filles s'emparent du rap." *L'Express* 26 Nov. 1998: 112–13.

Formula 2A2H. "Oxmo Puccino." *Radikal* Jun. 1998: 22–24.

Fraisse, Arnaud. "Thérapie de groupe." *Groove* Dec. 1998: 16–17.

Handelman, David. "Sold on Ice." *Rolling Stone* 10 Jan. 1991: 34, 38–44, 76.

George, Nelson. *Hip-Hop America*. New York: Viking, 1998.

Hip-Hop. TF1 [Télévision Française 1]. Narr. Sidney. Produced by Laurence Touitou. 1984–1985.

Jehli, David. "La croisade des NAP." *L'Affiche* Dec. 1998: 52.

"Joey Starr condamné à six mois fermes." 16 Jun. 1999. www.france2.fr/infos-gen/news-fr/112.htm (no longer accessible).

Kassovitz, Mathieu, dir. *La Haine*. Les Productions Lazennec, 1995.

Keita, David. "Solo. Le destin d'une non-star." *Radikal* Jul.-Aug. 1998: 22.

———. "Driver. Mister Funky Man." *Radikal* Sept. 1998: 15.

Laville, Alain. "Vu, Lu et Entendu." *Télé 7 Jours* 11–17 May 1996: 128.

Leland, John, and Marcus Mabry, with Dana Thomas. "Toasting the ŒHood." *Newsweek* 26 Feb. 1996: 42–43.

Lepoutre, David. *Coeur de banlieue. Codes, rites et langages*. Paris: Éditions Odile Jacob, 1997.

Louis, Patrick, and Laurent Prinaz. *Skinheads, Taggers, Zulus & Co*. Paris: La Table Ronde, 1990.

Night, Michael. "Sté. One in a Million." *Radikal* Nov. 1998: 26.

Mortaigne, Véronique. "L'industrie française du disque en recul en 1999." *Le Monde* 27 Jan. 2000. www.lemonde.fr/article-impression0.2322.396999.00.html (no longer accessible).

Peigne-Giuly, Annick. "Rencontre avec l'animateur de *Hip-Hop*, émission créée en 1984 sur TF1. Une date." *Libération* 23 Apr. 1996: 34.

Pliskin, Fabrice. "Oxmo Puccino. Black Cyrano." *Le Nouvel Observateur* 16–22 Jul. 1998: 27.

Prévos, André J. M. "Hip-Hop, Rap, and Repression in France and in the U.S." *Popular Music and Society* 22.2 (1998): 67–84.

———. "The Evolution of French Rap Music and Hip-Hop Culture in the 1980s and 1990s." *The French Review* 69.5 (1996): 713–25.

———. "Le 'mouvement alternatif,' un renouveau de la chanson populaire française? Le cas de 'Bérurier Noir' et des 'Garçons Bouchers'." *Contemporary French Civilization* 15.1 (1991): 35–51.

Puma, Clyde. *Le rap français*. Paris: Éditions Hors Collection, 1997.

Rockwell, John. "Felicitous Rhymes and Local Roots." *The New York Times* 23 Aug. 1992: 2:23.

Thibodat, Jean-Pierre. "Afrika Bambaataa roi zoulou du Bronx." *Libération* 28 Oct. 1982: 21.

Touraine, Emmanuelle, and Michel Marizy. "MC Solaar. Le rappeur nostalgique." *Télé 7–Jours* 26 Dec. 1997–3 Jan. 1998: 104–105.

Vulbeau, Alain. *Du tag au tag*. Paris: Desclée de Brouwer, 1992.

Zobel, Joseph. *Black Shack Alley* (*La rue Case-Nègres*). 1974. Trans. Keith Q. Warner. Washington, D.C.: Three Continents Press, 1980.

DISCOGRAPHY

Alliance Ethnik. *Simple et Funky*. Delabel, 1995.

Assassin. *Le futur que nous réserve-t-il?* 2 vols. Assassin Productions—Delabel, 1992.

Benny B., with DJ Daddy K & Perfect. *Perfect, Daddy K et Moi*. On The Beat Records, 1992.

Bérurier Noir. *Souvent fauché, toujours marteau*. Last Call, 1989.

BOSS. *BOSS, volume 2*. Epic, 2000.

Chagrin d'Amour. *Chagrin d'Amour*. Barclay, 1982.

CMP Familia. *L'honneur perdu*. Blanche Nègre Records, 1998.

Doc Gynéco. *Liaisons dangereuses*. Virgin/RUE, 1998.

———. *Première consultation*. Virgin, 1996.

Fabe. *Détournement de son*. Small Records, 1998.

———. *Le fond et la forme*. Mercury, 1997.

———. *Béfa surprend ses frères*. Mercury, 1995.

The Fabulous Trobadors. *Era pas de faire*, 1992.

IV My People. *IV My People. Certifié conforme*. MYP, 2000.

IAM. *Ombre est lumière*. Delabel, 1993.

Idéal J. *Le combat continue*. Barclay/Polygram, 1998.

Les Garçons Bouchers. *Les Garçons Bouchers, Tome 2*. Musidisc, 1989.

Les Inconnus. "Auteuil, Neuilly, Passy / C'est ton destin." Lederman, 1991.

KDD. *Opte pour le K*. Columbia Tristar, 1996.

LAMIFA. *Lamifa*. Musidisc, 1998.

——. *O.P.A. sur la rue*. Jimmy Jay Records-Arcade, 1996.

Les Little. *Les Vrais*. Mercury, 1992.

Lionel D. *Y a pas de problème*. Squatt, 1990.

Massilia Sound System. *Chourmo!* WMD, 1993.

MC Solaar. *Qui sème le vent récolte le tempo*. Polydor, 1991.

Mélaaz. *Mélaaz*. BMG, 1996.

Ministère AMER. *Pourquoi tant de haine?* Musidisc, 1992.

Manau. *Panique celtique*. Polydor, 1998.

Ménélik. *Je me souviens*. SOULCIETY, 1997.

——. *Phénoménélik*. SOULCIETY, 1995.

NAP. *La fin du monde*. RCA, 1998.

Oxmo Puccino. *Opéra Puccino*. Delabel, 1998.

Reciprok. *Il y a des jours comme ça*. Epic, 1996.

Rapattitudes. Labelle Noir/Virgin, 1989.

Rapattitudes 2. Rap et Reggae. Delabel, 1992.

Saï Saï. *Reggae Dance Hall*. WMD, 1992.

Saliha. *Résolument féminin*. Epic, 1994.

——. *Unique*. Virgin, 1991.

Sens Unik. *Les Portes du temps*. Unik Records, 1993.

Sté Strausz. *Ma Génération*. Delabel, 1998.

Suprême NTM. *Paris sous les bombes*. Sony/Epic, 1995.

——. *1993 . . . J'appuie sur la gâchette*. Epic, 1993.

——. *Authentik*. Epic, 1991.

Tonton David. *Allez leur dire*. Delabel, 1994.

Le Blues des racailles. Delabel, 1991.

Tout Simplement Noir. *Dans Paris nocturne*. Panam' Productions-Night & Day, 1995.

Yazid. *Je suis l'Arabe*. 1996.

2

Musical Dimensions and Ways of Expressing Identity in French Rap: The Groups from Marseilles

Jean-Marie Jacono
Translated from the French by Paul Rogers

Rap has developed in France mainly around two cities: Paris (and its suburbs) and Marseilles. Thanks to the group IAM's success, Marseilles has become a particularly dynamic rap scene that has given birth to several other groups now renowned in France, such as La Fonky Family, Le Troisième Oeil, and Faf Larage. IAM's fame was ensured not only by the themes of songs that often bring out the Marseilles identity or by the incredible presence on stage of the rappers in concert. It was also due to the high quality of the musical work of a band that not only has a DJ as one of its members, but also a "musical architect," a unique combination in French rap. The study of the musical dimensions of IAM and of the relationship between text and music is of great significance and fully justifies a musicological approach.

Yet, in this essay I will analyze to what extent the music conveys the expression of the Marseilles identity, which runs right through IAM's early texts. I will also try to find out if there is any trace of these musical dimensions in the creations of other groups from Marseilles. In other words, I will seek to establish the existence of a Marseilles style in French rap based on music. But answering this question is not easy. IAM no longer claim their Marseilles roots in their last album (1997). Nor can this claim always be found in the albums of the main rap groups from Marseilles. How important is the place of music, then, in this phenomenon? Can one say that the musical processes keep on expressing by themselves a form of the Marseilles identity that no longer exists in the words of the songs? For this analysis I will use the most significant albums of the main rap groups from Marseilles: IAM's three albums, *De la planète Mars* (From Planet Mars) (1991), *Ombre est Lumière* (Shadow Is Light) (1993), and *L'école du micro d'argent* (The Silver Microphone School) (1997); *Si Dieu veut* (If God Wants) by La Fonky Family (1997); *Hier, aujourd'hui, demain* (Yesterday, Today, Tomorrow) by Le Troisième Oeil (1999); and *C'est ma cause* (It's My Cause) by Faf Larage (Kif Kif Prod, 1998).[1] All these albums became hits. Therefore, they can be considered as particularly representative.

IAM: A GROUP OF REBELS FROM MARSEILLES

The group appeared in 1989 and built its image on a new vision of Marseilles, very different from the traditional picture taken from Provençal folklore. The great Mediterranean port is indeed famous all over France for the expansive and entertaining way of behaving of its inhabitants, popularized through Marcel Pagnol's films in the 1930s.[2] But above all, in France, Marseilles is the victim of a bad reputation. The city is generally regarded as dirty, violent, and full of dangers. In the public opinion, it remains the city of gangsters, the city of the "French connection."[3] It is also a big cosmopolitan port with large numbers of immigrants from Italy, and from former French colonies such as Algeria. Marseilles is the gateway to the Orient, a border metropolitan area where Africa begins. The city has lost the splendor that its port and its industrial activity directed towards the French colonies had generated up until the middle of the twentieth century. The result of the economic crisis of the 1970s was an increase in unemployment: an estimated 25% of the working population was out of work in 1986—much more than anywhere else in France (Morel, 128).[4] That crisis could not be solved despite the development of new activities and the emergence of a metropolis that now spreads beyond the administrative boundaries of the city. Marseilles has lost part of its inhabitants and its population is only 800,000 people according to the latest census (1999). Many young people of African origin live there and are the victims of poor academic performance, drugs, and unemployment. Racial and social tensions are high. Yet Marseilles has never experienced the kind of urban riots that periodically break out in the suburbs of other large French cities, for instance after the death of a youth "killed by mistake" by the police during an identity check.

The city represents a world in and of itself. Marseilles is surrounded by hills that delimit a very vast area (23,000 hectares), twice as big as that of Paris. Unlike Paris, however, the city has practically no suburbs. Although Marseilles is divided in two, with its poor districts in the north and its residential districts in the south, its inhabitants have much in common: they share the pleasures of the sea in summer and are enthusiastic fans of the OM (Olympique de Marseille), the city's professional soccer club, winner of the European Champions League in 1993. In Marseilles, at all levels of society, people feel that their city is the victim of the French government favoritism for Paris. It is a widely held idea among the inhabitants of the city that they belong to a particular world, distinct from Provence, that is the region around Marseilles. It is a world in which a typical accent in the pronunciation of French and special linguistic expressions play a key role, a world that finds its roots in the Mediterranean and the South, and that feels more closely related to the other Mediterranean cities than to the French capital.

It is precisely in that social and mental context that IAM was formed at the end of the 1980s, at a time when rap was very marginal in France. The group's name symbolizes their attachment to Marseilles. The meaning of it is, of course, first of all, "I am," but it can also be read as "Imperial Asiatic Men," or even "Invasion arrivant de Mars" (Invasion Coming from Mars) (Deroin, 30), where Marseilles is identified with the planet Mars to emphasize its specificity. The origin of the six members of the group is a mirror image of the ethnic composition of the city.[5] Blacks and whites play music side by side, which is usually not the case in American rap groups, and yet all of IAM's members are foreigners or of foreign origin. IAM's strength lies in their ability to progressively combine rap, an American social and artistic expression, with the reality of Marseilles. The notion of "interstitial culture," that is to say, the young people's culture emerging between the culture of the immigration country and that of the country from which their parents come, is essential here.[6] It is the "hidden" face of the city that the group will highlight, what they call its "dark side," which is so detrimental to the city, and something you are not supposed to talk about. This dark side is totally opposed to the traditional picture of Marseilles, which does not tally with the rappers': "Le temps du Provençal rigolo est révolu" (The days of funny Provençal are in the past), IAM asserts in the tune "Mars contre-attaque" (Mars Counter-Attacks) (*Ombre est lumière, vol. 1*).

IAM's members see themselves as urban witnesses. They denounce the violence of the city, drugs, the rising threat of racism and of the National Front,[7] the politicians' lack of concern for the fate of the poorest. Like the American rappers they met several times in New York even before the band formed, they take a firm stand. The influence of the American afro-centrism was important at the beginning. You find it in the Egyptian names of IAM's members. It puts Marseilles back in the context of African civilizations. It identifies, in a mythical way, the city going through a crisis with civilizations jeopardized by the evolution of the world. The references to ancient Egypt are obvious throughout the first two albums and they go hand in hand with the evocation of Marseilles. It is particularly unique in French rap, which actually emerged in 1989, thanks to a compilation—*Rapattitudes*—made by a small independent label bringing rap and ragamuffin groups together, while IAM was beginning to make its name in concerts before Marseilles audiences. This new tone comes out in IAM's first album, *De la planète Mars* (1991), one of the first key albums in French rap. But above all, IAM's success was materialized with their double album *Ombre est Lumière* (1993).

One of the titles of the album, "Je danse le mia" (I Dance the Mia) tells, in a funny way, about the evenings the youths used to spend in Marseilles nightclubs in the 1980s. This song had a tremendous success, and in 1994 it became a big hit all over France. It was then that rap music for the first time spread to an audience different from the suburban youths. The "Mia" confirmed the celebration throughout France of the new Marseilles identity, which allowed people to be proud of being from Marseilles. The city was rediscovered. Because of its cultural vitality, the expression "Marseilles *movida*" was used. Yet the success of the "Mia" proved to be ambiguous. It led to another picturesque vision of Marseilles, to a new folklore. It also overshadowed the most significant titles of the album, and the musical work of a group that was expressing the identity of the city in an original way. To examine this music means to consider rap not only as a sociological expression but also as an artistic expression.

THE POWER OF THE MUSICAL DIMENSIONS

We cannot talk about the music without mentioning the themes the group deals with. *Ombre est lumière* is the album that reveals the richest subjects. Criticizing the social life and developing IAM's ideas are the main lines of an album in which Marseilles is already not referred to as often as in *De la planète Mars* (Kosmicki, 93–108). Fewer titles actually evoke Marseilles. But in fact the oppositions and contrasts of this city deprived of urban homogeneity can be found in the very diversity of subjects. IAM's strength lies in their conception of a musical structure in which the variety of themes is highlighted by two alternating types of titles: songs and inserts. The latter are small snatches, generally very funny and full of coinages. These inserts create a pause, but also restart the listening process. What is striking in IAM, is how they play with forms to bring a rhythmic dimension to the structure of the album. For instance, the nineteen titles of the first volume of *Ombre est Lumière* are arranged according to a structure in which songs and inserts are distributed in a regular way, with three songs followed by an insert, then three more songs and an insert, etc.

Of course this structure is not found in every album. Yet the insert functions as a means of passing between two different groups of songs. Its use is not left to chance. We have surmised that it could be seen as a metaphor of space in the city of Marseilles, where opposite sections are connected to each other by shortcuts (Jacono, 1999: 109–19). The inserts also reveal a great deal of linguistic and literary treasures, not only in IAM's albums but also in those of a renowned ragamuffin group in Marseilles, the Massilia Sound System. It represents the expression of a local oral identity that does not use the same registers of language that are used in songs (Gasquet-Cyrus, 121–47).

The kind of French spoken in Marseilles is very seldom referred to in IAM's texts. The vocabulary includes practically no endogenous expressions deriving from Provençal. In IAM's verse, the language used is "standard" French, in which mainly appear neologisms coined by the group (Calvet, 1999: 57–71). So the contrasting effects that reveal the Marseilles identity are conveyed by declamation. Akhenaton and Shurik'n, the two rappers of the group, who often sing together, do not have the same "flow." Shurik'n generally stresses the syllables of the words on the second and the fourth beats. These syllables correspond to the beats stressed by the rhythm in a quadruple time bar that represents an essential landmark to rappers. Akhenaton has a more varied type of stressing, in which the stress may fall on the first and third beats. This declamation in permanent motion often results in technically brilliant passages. A rapper usually does not organize his declamation of a line within the limits of a single quadruple time bar. His flow drives him to go beyond this metrical frame. In general, the end of the line and the end of the bar (fourth beat) coincide after two or three bars (Jacono, 1998: 65–75). In IAM, it can occur after five or six bars, or even more, such as in the tune "Demain, c'est loin," (Tomorrow Is Far) (*L'école du micro d'argent*).

Moreover, this flow, never steady, is different in each of IAM's two rappers. These contrasts are sometimes intensified by the use of snatches of non-declaimed text inside the scanned text. These snatches are expressions of everyday life. A good example can be found in "L'aimant" (The Magnet), a song talking about the life of someone living in a housing project of Marseilles, in which greetings appear in the flow from the very beginning of the song: "J'ai commencé à vivre ma vie dans les poubelles dans un quartier de camés où les blattes craquent sous tes semelles. *Salut-salut, ça va*. Les mecs observent ta voiture neuve. (*Ombre est lumière, vol. 1*)[8]

This quotation from everyday language, very original in French rap, is only one of the processes used by IAM in their songs to vary their declamation (Jacono, 1999: 109–19). However, the greatest diversity is to be found in their use of samples. This kind of work, that can be labeled orchestration, has no equivalent in rap.

The use of samples from very different kinds of music and sources is characteristic of IAM's work. These samples are connected with the meaning of the text. IAM's songs contain numerous extracts from traditional music, especially in the *intros* (introductions). In the album *Ombre est lumière*, a tune is played on the raita (an Arabic instrument that has similarities to the oboe) at the beginning of "J'aurais pu croire" (I Could Have Believed), a song about the Gulf War; there is a tune on the mandolin in "Où sont les roses ?" (Where Are the Roses ?), a song about the Italian immigration in Provence; and, in *L'école du micro d'argent*, one can hear a Balinese gamelan at the beginning of the album.

IAM also borrows music from films ("Pharaon revient" [The Return of the Pharaoh] in *Ombre est lumière*) or dialogues taken from films ("L'empire du côté obscur" [The Empire of the Dark Side] in *L'école du micro d'argent*), as well as other musical sources: French songs such as Serge Gainsbourg's "Harley Davidson" (*Ombre est lumière, vol. 1*); American famous tunes such as George Benson's "Give Me the Night," sampled in "Je danse le mia" (*Ombre est lumière, vol. 1*); natural sounds like those of the ocean in "Le repos c'est la santé" (Resting Is Healthy) (*Ombre est lumière, vol. 2*); sound effects, like war noises in "Le soldat," (The Soldier) (*Ombre est lumière, vol. 1*), and finally, a duo with American rappers Wu-Tang Clan in "La saga" (*L'école du micro d'argent*).

Furthermore, IAM's work is not merely centered on the choice of samples. For each title, their work on the sound is significant as well. The use of pauses ("J'aurais pu croire," "L'empire du côté obscur") creates a break in rhythm that gives dynamism to the flow. IAM's concern for varying the musical dimensions continuously on a strongly marked basic rhythm is also obvious when it comes to the form. For instance, the famous hit "Je danse le mia" is built upon a regular structure (versechorus); instead of the chorus, at a decisive moment in the song there is a disco announcement right before a repeat in which the flow is totally new. In IAM, you even find a rhythm organized on seven time ("Le 7," in *Ombre est lumière, vol. 1*), which is unique in rap.

THE EVOLUTION OF IDENTITY

Consequently, IAM's musical work is based on a great variety of means and processes. The group often exploits breaks in rhythm, in declamation, and in orchestration to indicate differences. Their refusal to create a homogeneous musical world thanks to the presence of numerous contrasts is linked with their assertion of the Marseilles identity. It is exactly as if IAM represents the musical form of the geographic, ethnic, and cultural diversity of the city itself. Marseilles binds together its inhabitants beyond the cultures of their countries of origin. Through its rap music, IAM unifies musical sources that could not meet elsewhere.

The group's intention to express the Marseilles identity in its music has nevertheless evolved. The contrasting effects are less exploited in *L'école du micro d'argent*. The album no longer contains inserts, and the samples are less varied, except in the titles quoted above. The rhythm is more regular. In fact, IAM chooses to go back to the fundamentals of rap, that is the power of speech on a sober musical background (Kosmicki, 106). The last title, "Demain c'est loin" (Tomorrow Is Far), lasts nine minutes and symbolizes this orientation. This is a French rap masterpiece that is based on the linking of the declamations of both rappers.

THE NEW GENERATION

Marseilles is no longer evoked on an album in which music is emphasized as well as social criticism. Nevertheless, IAM's influence is evident in other groups from Marseilles who also use a good number of contrasting effects. The new generation in Marseilles rap actually emerged after the success of *Ombre est lumière* in 1994. The new groups have tried to find their own way. For instance, Faf Larage (brother of IAM's Shurik'n) no longer talks about Marseilles in *C'est ma cause*. La Fonky Family denounces the living conditions in Marseilles, but most of all they stand for the identity of Belsunce, an "Arabic" district of ill repute situated in downtown Marseilles. As for Le Troisième Oeil, they talk about the many young immigrants from the Comoro Islands living in the housing projects of the northern districts of the city. However, for each of these groups, Marseilles remains a city in which the youths from the housing projects are the victims of violence, drugs, and unemployment. The lyrics often deal with these subjects, but they contain no trace of the mysticism linked with Ancient Egypt, and are less varied than those written by IAM. The music, too, is not as diversified as that of the great Marseilles group. Yet it contains numerous contrasts in the choice of the samples and in their use, as well as in their conception of "musical flow."

IAM's influence is perceptible in Faf Larage, who gives a particular sound to each title. His album contains extremely varied rhythmic or melodic samples from string instruments, keyboards, or film soundtracks, but also dazzling scratches that interfere with the declaimed text. The ninth title of the album, "A l'arraché" (With Much Effort) (*C'est ma cause*), opens with a series of very different musical moments, imitating the style of IAM. These quick changes create a constant variation of the flow, due to the presence of several rappers (La Fonky Family, K. Ryme Le Roi). Other rappers also appear as special guests on other titles, IAM for instance ("J'accuse" [I Accuse]). On Faf Larage's tunes, the presence of dialogues contrasting with the flow is another sign of IAM's influence ("C'est ma cause," "Le rapublicain" [The Rapublican (sic)]).

Le Troisième Oeil's album reveals a great diversity of samples too. Among others, they quote television series (introduction of "La Boomba"), Zao, the Congolese singer ("La guerre" [The War]), or Johann Sebastian Bach ("Hymne à la Racaille" [Hymn to the Rogues]). Several passages in the language of the Comoros create a special atmosphere in the album, as in "Eldorado," which tells the story of the immigrants who originally came from this Indian Ocean island to Marseilles. The flow itself is renewed by the presence of several rappers, of dialogues, and of screams ("Manipule" [Manipulate]).

La Fonky Family's style of expression is based on the contrasts of varying types of declamation inside a brisk and vigorous flow. The numerous guest rappers increase this diversity, as in "Marseille envahit" (Marseilles Invades), in which Le Troisième Oeil is featured. Here, the introductions and the inserts (called "verse" in the album) showcase the greatest variety of samples, as in "Les mains sales" (The Dirty Hands). Even if this variety of musical techniques may be used by other groups, in Marseilles, it takes on particular importance. The systematic use of such methods is not only a direct heritage from IAM, but also the expression of the Marseilles diversity. It is just as if the groups of the new generation had kept that need for a diversified expression in orchestration as well as in declamation. Therefore, it is clear that some of the fundamental aspects of IAM's style have been preserved.

The new generation in Marseilles rap keeps using some of IAM's musical techniques. Based on the increase in the number of vocal and rhythmic contrasts and on the use of original samples in the music, these methods are evidence of the presence of a city that is by nature the product of differences. Can one say, then, that a Marseilles style in rap actually exists? The differences between the groups are patent, but there are also striking similarities. Only an exhaustive study of the production of all the Marseilles groups would make the definition of a style possible. Above all, rap is a form of expression that emanates from a specific place, even though it can be of universal significance: "IAM is a Marseilles group. . . . We could not do the same in another place. You take IAM, you put them in Paris, it does not work anymore" (Deroin et al., 30). As a result, identity is not claimed through the words only. It is not only a matter of religion, of ethnic (the expression of a minority) or social origin, of generation (the youths), or even of geography (the fact of belonging to a city or a district). It also reveals itself through music, which plays a determining role from this point of view, and as a result, as we have seen, identity and Maseilles rap lyrics have become closely intertwined.

NOTES

1. I have left aside titles by less famous groups, brought together in such compilations as *Chroniques de Mars*, *Face cachée de Mars*, as well as the personal productions of the members of IAM group.

2. See the famous Marseilles trilogy, *Marius* (1931), *Fanny* (1932), and *César* (1936).

3. This bad image is also due to the successful Holywood motion pictures starring Gene Hackman, *The French Connection* (1971), and its sequel, *The French Connection II* (1975). Both films deal with drug smuggling in Marseilles.

4. The highest unemployment rate in France was about 14% (Morel, 128).

5. "Chill," known as Akhenaton (Philippe Fragione), grandson of a Neapolitan immigrant, and "Shurik'n Chang-Ti" (Geoffroy Mussard), black of Malagasy origin, rappers. "Kheops" (Eric Mazel), DJ of Spanish origin, and "Imhotep" (Pascal Perez), "musical architect," *pied-noir* (Algerian-born Frenchman), musicians. "Malek Sultan" (Malek Brahimi), Algerian, and "Kephren" (François Mendy), of Senegalese origin, dancers.

6. See Louis-Jean Calvet (1994: 269), Hugues Bazin, and Manuel Boucher.

7. A French extreme right political party.

8. Translation: "I began to live my life among the garbage cans in a place full of junkies where you crunch cockroaches under your soles at every step *Hi!—Hi! What's up?* The guys are checking out your car."

9. Parts of this chapter have appeared in *Pardes et musiques à Mouséilles* (eds. Médéric Gasquet-Cyrus et al., L'Harmattan, 1999). I thank the publisher for permission to use that material here.

WORKS CITED

Bazin, Hugues. *La Culture Hip-Hop*. Paris: Desclée de Brouwer, 1995.

Boucher, Manuel. *Rap, expression des lascars. Signification et enjeux du rap dans la société française*. Paris: L'Harmattan, 1998.

Calvet, Louis-Jean. "L'endogène, l'exogène et la néologie: le lexique marseillais." In *Paroles et musiques à Marseille*. Eds. Médéric Gasquet-Cyrus, Guillaume Kosmicki, and Cécile Van den Avenne. Paris: L'Harmattan, 1999. 57–71.

———. *Les Voix de la ville. Introduction à la sociolinguistique urbaine*. Paris: Payot, 1994.

César. Dir. Marcel Pagnol. Les Films Marcel Pagnol, 1936.

Deroin, Didier, Fred Guilledoux, Stéphan Muntaner, and Gilles Rof. *IAM. Le livre*. Toulon: Soleil Productions—Plein Sud, 1996.

Fanny. Dir. Marc Allégret. Les Films Marcel Pagnol, 1932.

The French Connection. Dir. William Friedkin. 20th Century Fox, 1971.

The French Connection II. Dir. John Frankenheimer. 20th Century Fox, 1975.

Gasquet-Cyrus, Médéric. "Les inserts dans le rap et le raggamuffin marseillais." In *Paroles et musiques à Marseille*. Eds. Médéric Gasquet-Cyrus, Guillaume Kosmicki, and Cécile Van den Avenne. Paris: L'Harmattan, 1999. 121–47.

Gasquet-Cyrus, Médéric, Guillaume Kosmicki, and Cécile Van der Avenne, eds. *Paroles et Musiques à Marseille*. Paris: L'Harmattan, 1999.

Jacono, Jean-Marie. "Les dimensions musicales des chansons d'IAM, éléments d'un rap méditerranéen." In *Paroles et musiques à Marseille*. Eds. Médéric Gasquet-Cyrus, Guillaume Kosmicki, and Cécile Van den Avenne. Paris: L'Harmattan, 1999. 109–19.

———. "Pour une analyse des chansons de rap." *Musurgia* 5.2 (1998): 65–75.

———. "Le rap français: inventions musicales et enjeux sociaux d'une création populaire." In *La Musique depuis 1945—Matériau, Esthétique et Perception*. Eds. Joël-Marie Fauquet and Hugues Dufourt. Liège: Mardaga, 1996. 45–60.

Kosmicki, Guillaume. "L'évolution du groupe IAM: un parcours thématique et musical sensé." In *Paroles et musiques à Marseille*. Eds. Médéric Gasquet-Cyrus, Guillaume Kosmicki, and Cécile Van den Avenne. Paris: L'Harmattan, 1999. 93–108.

Marius. Dirs. Alexandre Korda and Marcel Pagnol. Les Films Marcel Pagnol, 1931.

Morel, Bernard. *Marseille—Naissance d'une métropole*. Paris: L'Harmattan, 1999.

DISCOGRAPHY

Benson, George. "Give Me the Night." *Give Me the Night*. WEA/Warner Brothers, 1980.

Faf Larage. *C'est ma cause*. Kif Kif Productions, 1998.

La Fonky Family. *Si Dieu veut*. Sony Music, 1997.

Gainsbourg, Serge. "Harley Davidson (Palace 80)." *De Serge Gainsbourg à Gainsbarre*. 2 vols. Philips/Mercury, 1980.

IAM. *L'école du micro d'argent*. Delabel, 1997.

———. *Ombre est lumière*. 2 vols. Delabel, 1993.

———. *De la planète Mars*. Labelle Noir/Virgin, 1991.

Rapattitudes. Labelle Noir/Virgin, 1989.

Le Troisième Oeil. *Hier, aujourd'hui, demain*. Columbia, 1999.

Various Artists. *Chroniques de Mars*. BMG, 1998.

———. *Face cachée de Mars*. Globe Music, 1999.

3

Common Partitions: Musical Commonplaces[1]

Anthony Pecqueux
Translated from the French by Yannick Nassoy
and Seth Whidden

Both on records and on stage, there are commonplaces about rap, especially about its various practices; these commonplaces will be called "common partitions," in the sense of separate plans of action. They serve to express first a particular knowledge of the art world of rap (of the history of its practices, actors, and constituent rules and a partisan position on the latter), and then the existence of a social, emotive, or cognitive relationship between artists and audiences. It is from this angle, and in a perspective borrowed from pragmatics from a socio-anthropological point of view, that I will examine some expressions of that relationship, which underlies the skills required to practice and appreciate this music. To do so, it must be posited that musical activity contains its very introduction onto the public scene: it takes on the procedural form of the test.[2] The latter represents the fundamental process by which an artist, in support of the previous tests, ventures to confront his own ideal of rap—actualized by his practice—with that of listeners.[3]

MUSICAL NONCHALANCE

As a general rule, rappers[4] establish and put to the test a relationship with audiences. In order to characterize them more precisely, let us consider the distinction the actors agree to make between "the underground" and "the general public," the former referring to "our audience, that is those who listen to hip-hop" and the latter to "everyman." The aim between those two groups is quite plain: "When I speak of people, obviously I mean the general public" (*Groove*). It amounts to distinguishing "*amateurs*"[5] from "the-greatest-possible-number-of-people." The *amateurs* are those who enjoy rap productions and let it be known by buying them, and those who like rap and let it be known by always being potential *amateur*-practitioners—and not necessarily "bands," the necessary condition consisting of uttering words to a preexistent tune.

As for the-greatest-possible-number-of-people, it consists of those who are also likely to buy these productions for it is "a type of music that is not intended for a hundred people but for millions of them."[6] If the-greatest-possible-number-of-people must be aimed at, it remains to be determined what the rappers' target is; that is, which of the two groups are concerned. Here I am taking up the distinction made by Jacques Cheyronnaud between "two different operations: taking someone or something as one's target (this will be called targeting), and using this designation of a target to some purpose (this will be called aiming)" ("La raillerie," 78). Yet, on the one hand, *amateurs* are never won beforehand and by definition the-greatest-possible-number-of-people always remains to be won; on the other hand, it is impossible to address (segments of) songs to each of these two groups separately. As a result, rappers always target them both at the same time; the distinction between these two categories does not hold as far as the singing activity is concerned. I may now define the fact of addressing them both at the same time as targeting those concerned, that is, through a single musical act addressing the *amateurs* and treating the-greatest-possible-number-of-people as concerned ones. These being "individuals who minimally converge on expectations regarding the practices of rap" (Cheyronnaud, "La grand-messe," 32) and who feel neither forgotten nor betrayed by the fact that priority is given to sales.

Any distinction must thus be abandoned and only one category is worth retaining: namely, those concerned. And among them no one is unaware that they contribute to this procedural form: being concerned means accepting to contribute to it and ratifying it, and vice versa. Nor is anyone unaware of the fact that a form of nonchalance gradually comes to prevail among them all—some targeting concerned ones, others being put on an equal footing with a priori nonconcerned ones, others knowing that their status has been raised. This nonchalance stems from a general attitude of rappers that they have to communicate with ostentation; this attitude will be referred to as "self-irony." I will not take up the classic analyses regarding this is-

sue because I do not view this attitude as the fact of uttering P in order to communicate non-P, even though this also exists. Self-irony
can be found in the communication of a relationship with concerned
ones and consists of a critical distance from oneself and what one
does, and accordingly from the listeners who appreciate these practices. This self-ironic nonchalance does not denote a lack of seriousness in one's work, but on the contrary a concentration on the lack of
seriousness required in targeting concerned ones.

Neither does it correspond to a lack of respect for listeners since it
results in strategically making use of their perspicacity; they become
concerned only when they understand this nonchalance. The use that
comes from them extends to all kinds of inferences, interpretations,
and conclusions on the basis of the hypothesis contained in this target: "If you really are hip-hop, you know quite well what we're talking about; you're therefore in a position to fill in the blanks, to understand by yourself." While it is rarely formulated in this way,[7] it
nonetheless remains implied all the time. For instance, when the
Fonky Family say "No model, we all try to find ourselves a place / If
God wants one day we too will hold . . ." ("La vie de rêve" [The
Dream Life]), it is the listener who completes the sentence with "a
place," which is not mentioned in the song, especially as s/he is supposed to know that the group's first album, entitled *si Dieu Vent* [If
God Wants], enabled them to somehow hold "a place."

DISCOGRAPHIC PARTITIONS

A record may be considered an anamorphosis of a musical action: a reduction of a life-size practice to the size of this material medium,
which is also a necessary stage in the relationship with a public since
ours is a culture of sound antecedence. I will now try to find a few instances of this musical nonchalance from the angle of common partitions, which are as many creative repetitions (that is, keyings of original schemas). The act of "referring to something" is an interesting
starting point, since reference is all about how to make it clear that ut-
terances concern a particular field of reality: how to render the words-
world direction of fit, as John Robert Searle puts it (3). This relationship between words and the world fits into the meta-relationship
between the co-communicators; therefore noticing the references in a

speech allows one to grasp some elements of this self-irony. For reference implies a global process of selecting from among the objects in the world, of taking a stand on them, of addressing the co-communicator, and of qualifying all these operations. These all make it necessary to let some intention show; one does not refer to anything in just any old way, especially since self-irony as a way of putting the perspicacity of the co-communicator to the test often contains a clause of referential vagueness. Therefore, it is up to the latter to decide on an interpretation. These references may concern the geographical environment, wanderings that are common practices in cities (or in a city); the social and political, or cultural environment; leisure activities—commonplaces about celebration or boredom are then involved; etc. The most striking references are those that allude to common partitions of the practice of rap, and that can be either universal or local.

Local and Supposedly Common to Some of Those Concerned by French Rap

Bringing controlled derision to its height, Stomy Bugsy turned a hit entitled "Bad boys de Marseille" into "Le playboy de Sarcelles."[8] In addition to the pun in the title and the thematic changes he made, he chose two M.C.s from the original version for the choirs. And above all, he chose as a musical basis the tune that Ennio Morricone composed for the film *Le Professionnel* (The Professional). In France, this tune is less associated with the motion picture than with a television commercial for Royal Canin dog food, in which a dog, radiant with health, runs in the mountains. By slowing the tune, he conjures up this dog in the act of running and cannot fail to suggest a sort of identification with him; this is a very curious playboy indeed.

References may be limited within a school, such as that of the "silver microphone" brought to life by IAM in Marseilles (IAM). One of its watchwords is the phrase "a type of music that is not intended for a hundred people but for millions of them," which according to the same M.C. becomes: "a joint not that is not intended for a hundred people but for my lungs / Precisely for my lungs!" (Akhenaton, Freeman, et al.). These local references may ultimately become a self-referential and especially self-ironic play of mirrors. Such is the case with Faf Larage, who imagined an interview of a do-nothing who lives off of his girlfriend's salary; the problem is that "there was this rapper on TV one night; the guy is not bad, actually. His name is Faf Larage. He's my spitting image, my girlfriend thought it was I (. . .). She bought the album of Kheops [on which this very song plays], on which I'm supposed to rap. That guy's got some nerve! (. . .) He wrote a text and it sounds like a more vulgar version of myself" (Faf Larage).

Universal and Synecdoches of the Act of Rapping

Let us take the famous example "Yes yes yo / On the beat yo." Repeating it is not enough; it has to be skillfully modeled above all. According to Faf Larage, the do-nothing who wants to tell his life story through rap goes: "Wech wech yo / On my bed yo." One of the historic origins of rap, the ego-trip, becomes the "megotrip" (Akhenaton, Freeman, et al.)[9] in a hymn to marijuana.

Universal and Situated in a Particular Context

This is a fundamental type of reference which makes it possible to complete the process of targeting concerned ones, with the system of judgement in the context of a concert—a specificity of rap: "Raise your hand, your fist and your joint if you recognize yourself," "Raise your fist, raise your joint, raise your head my friend," and "Raise your hand if you're hip-hop / And say la la la la."[10] These injunctions in the form of guides for action indeed make it possible to complete the action that started by targeting concerned ones; people who had never been to a rap concert before would then become competent, as they would find out that they cover the reality of the system of judgement applied here.

Stage Partitions

This last reference leads me to move on to concerts and to the common partitions put into play there. A concert will again be defined as the procedural form of the test, which seems fairly archetypal at first sight but certainly deserves further discussion. As a process that contains the clause of its judgement—a process that includes this judgement's expression—it represents the place par excellence where a taste can be expressed. Hannah Arendt, in a commentary of Kant's *Critique of Judgement*, defined this act in this way:

> Judgement, to be valid, depends on the presence of others. (. . .) That the capacity to judge is a specifically political ability in exactly the sense denoted by Kant, namely, the ability to see things not only from one's own point of view but in the perspective of all those who happen to be present; (. . .) Judging is one, if not the most, important activity in which this sharing-the-world-with-others comes to pass. (221)

This taste is expressed through judgement but, as the author shows, the latter does not consist in approval or rejection but in co-approval or co-rejection, which is collectively made. A concert entails specific procedures of action that result from the commitment to something and with someone; in other words, it is an eminently political activity. That explains the particular institutional attention devoted to concerts; the assembly as such does not constitute a threat, for the threat stems from the procedures involved. For instance, when a civil servant in the City Hall of Marseilles read the relatively neutral review of a hip-hop festival in Marseilles in the daily newspaper *Libération*,[11] he concluded: "Organizers simply have to choose local groups because there is some pressure; otherwise these concerts would end badly (. . .). At the Marsatac festival, there were more than two thousand of them; there would have been big problems otherwise (. . .) it's specific to rap" (Mérit).

Besides, as I pointed out previously, ours is a culture of sound antecedence of a discographic nature, one of the implementations of which is to target concerned ones. Since in addition, its upshot is the reference to the system of judgement during concerts, I will posit that a concert gathers concerned ones; it configures and sustains a culture of concerned ones. On this basis, I will now describe a few of the partitions proposed by artists with a view of the felicity of the plan of action during my two series of ethnographical observations. The first one came within the context of a line-up of leading groups in French rap, centered on the concert given by Das EFX in a small music hall in the city center;[12] the second one was a hip-hop festival gathering the different modes of expression of hip-hop in several halls of a complex in an outlying area.[13] These partitions constitute acts of reference that touch on what follows.

The Social and Political Context, and at the Same Time They Refer to Prior Practices, in a Critical Schema of Institutional Denunciation

While the National Front (an extreme right-wing political party) remains one of the first targets of stigmatization, it is now stigmatized only according to particular circumstances generally speaking, its systematic denunciation being now too easy. On the other hand, the police keep this systematic character, which is often very effective to win the audience's support.

Abuse is not enough; groups still have to give an inventive show in which the audience can take part. For instance, the group IV My People first invited the audience at the Marsatac festival to raise their forefingers in the air and to sing the slogan "fuck the police"; those concerned ones, knowing the device all too well, did not react and some even snickered. One of the M.C.s had to arouse them by saying that wherever they had played, even in small towns, "when we say 'fuck the police,' the audience makes a hell of noise"; the audience complied on this second incitement. At the same festival, the D.J. of the group Prodige Namor started playing a piece that went "Houhou, houhou"; the concerned ones continued right away and spontaneously instead of KRS One: "That's the sound of da police!" This is indeed an instance of reference, of strategic use of the perspicacity of the concerned ones; this use makes the latter thoughtful again of collective political commitment against the institution of the police. My last example is also a referential one: in the line-up Das EFX, the group Puissance Nord played their song "Assassinat du poulet" (Murder of the Chicken)[14] only after asking if there were any police officers in the hall. This was a sort of judicial precaution with a testimonial effect; the group NTM had been sentenced in 1997 for insulting police officers who were present during a concert.

The Cultural and Emotional Contexts

A few partitions turn out to be quite useful for winning the support of an audience without lapsing into gratuitous flattery, which would be disapproved of by those concerned ones who "won't be taken in." For example, the M.C.'s Arabica at the Dream Team Gathering[15] played their first song amidst the total indifference of their audience; one of the

M.C.s even got angry with them. The second M.C. took the floor to introduce the second song, saying he was very glad that they were quiet since it was necessary to listen carefully to their lyrics, which were about the wasteland of North Africa. Moreover, he said that he dedicated the song to his mother, who had come to see him in concert for the first time then and who had known the wasteland before the Algerian civil war. Applause broke out, all the more so because the first M.C. had gotten hold of an Algerian flag and because the song was built on a sample of traditional Algerian music. They eventually received a standing ovation; it had taken these two essential emotional aspects represented by the figures of identity that are the mother and the wasteland to reverse a situation that had promised to be very delicate at first. There is another emotional aspect that is effective when adequately introduced: namely, letting a teenager or a child up on the stage. The Mafia Trece gladly did it at the Marsatac festival, causing dynamic surprise. The M.C.'s Arabica did not meet with as much success when they did it just after, for the element of surprise was over.

Commonplaces about Concerts, Which May Also Become Mistakes in the Adaptation to the Situation

These mistakes stem from an error in judgement either of the audience or of the frame of the performance and can even lead bands to give up playing live. Among the cases of the audience's errors, Cheb Aïssa tried to have the audience join in the chorus at the Marsatac festival; they were supposed to go "Ohohohohoh." This unsuccessful attempt was prolonged during three choruses without having the slightest effect. As for cases of misjudgment of the frame of the situation, I will take the example of the group KDD who, at the same festival, after having left the stage, came back a few minutes later and expressed their disappointment at the fact that the audience had not demanded an encore. But these concerned ones were fully aware of the format of the festival, where there is never any encore since a previously set program has to be followed; here it is the group who does not respect the format. And those mistakes are likely to lead groups to give up playing live, which above all means giving in to the audience's ultimate power of decision, as was the case with rapper Daddy Lord C. at the Marsatac festival. Indeed five minutes after the beginning of his performance, the hall had almost emptied out, and after fifteen minutes' silence on the part of the audience he asked if they wanted more of it: meeting with more silence he left the stage, though the average performance lasted for forty-five minutes.

These considerations suggest a few interesting leads for further analysis of the practices of rap and their cultural reception. On the one hand, they bring to light a few skills required to practice this music, through the mastery of the relevant uses of language. It is necessary to target concerned ones and to let self-irony plainly show, to proceed by more or less strong implications, especially by means of references containing a clause of interpretative ambiguity. But that is not the only means; nonchalance comes within the larger score of all the speeches that may be labeled as skillful and which, to reach pertinence, oscillate between literality and metaphorality in the context of a general stylistic line that rappers set for themselves and that remains inseparable from the idea of a continuum between literality and metaphorality (Pecqueux, 59–77).

On the other hand, it is necessary to make use of the listeners' perspicacity; in order to be able to appreciate this music (that is, its metaphors, literality, self-irony, references: in a word, to be concerned by it), one has to go through many interpretative procedures: inferences, hypotheses, etc. These are both necessary and sufficient, just as it is necessary and sufficient for rappers to make use of them. This means that these different skills are interdependent: they are co-required by those who practice this music and by those who listen to it, and continue to be collectively and gradually defined, relative to the minimal constituent rules of this art world.

That explains why this music contains so many common partitions and why they are so present in its studio-recorded as well as live performances; and above all it explains why rappers often stand on the narrow thread of those partitions, modulating them with many puns and much stage business. On the one hand those not concerned, who do not know about these constituent rules that are "played" with, cannot understand where the creative character lies and only notice repetitions: hence the impression of conformity and lack of originality often criticized (Pecqueux, 16–19). On the other hand, those concerned know about these partitions and consequently look for original musical actions, on the stage as well as on records. And that is where a great part of the interest of ethnographical observations of concerts lies; rappers certainly dare to establish a culture of concerned ones, but then they have to assume its practical consequences. For if the audience consists of concerned ones, it will also be the most difficult type of audience, one who "won't be taken in" and who will require the greatest effort so as to prevent plain disappointment.

NOTES

1. Support for the writing of this essay came from a grant awarded by the Provence Region (PACA) and the *'02 Q.P. de Mars* Association. This work is entirely aimed at proposing and putting to the test a few exploratory tools for an analysis of the practices of rap. It is the fruit of work supervised by Jean-Louis Fabiani and Jacques Cheyronnaud (Ph.D. at the E.H.E.S.S. in progress).

2. I use the term in its dynamic sense pointed out by Boltanski and Thévenot: the confrontation of an ideal or a theory with a public situation.

3. My discographical references come from an ordinary corpus for a listener of French rap; as for the references to concerts, they result from ethnographical observations carried out mainly at two series of concerts in Marseilles.

4. I will concentrate on M.C.s and on their performative evocations of what they do but I will bear in mind that the word "rappers" refers to them as well as to their musical counterparts, D.J.s. On the one hand, a song results from a certain relation between a tune and its lyrics. On the other hand, musical creation in rap consists of recycling a preexistent musical or cultural heritage in an original way; therefore D.J.s also put a relationship to the test of their listeners: namely, the relationship between this heritage and the resulting innovation.

5. The French word "amateur" means both "those who like something," or "fans" and "those who practice a music, or a sport, as an amateur" (as opposed to professionally). To preserve this double meaning (which is absent from its English counterpart), we have chosen to keep the original French word (translator's note).

6. Akhenaton (with La Fonky Family), "Bad boys de Marseille — version sauvage."

7. When it actually is, it is usually a pedagogical warning as in the case with Mos Def: "We are hip-hop, you, me, everybody, we are hip-hop so hip-hop is goin' where we're goin'."

8. Akhenaton (with La Fonky Family), "Bad boys de Marseille" and Stomy Bugsy, respectively.

9. Pun formed with the words "mégot" and "trip." "Mégot" is a colloquial word for "cigarette end" (translator's note).

10. La Fonky Family, "Sans titre"; Busta Flex, "Black" and "Hip-hop forever," respectively.

11. "A young and urban crowd invaded the Docks des Suds on Friday night, around seven p.m. (. . .) each night, more than two thousand people turned up (. . .) some members of the audience had gotten in despite a quite burdensome team of bouncers (. . .). Rap has achieved parity with reggae as the emblematic music of the popular districts of Marseille, so much so that the organizers say it is impossible not to make way for local formations." The journalist simply wanted to point out that it is difficult to overlook the vitality of local practices; the audience has nothing to do with it, those concerts being organized and their programs being set well in advance.

12. May 19, 2000, at the Espace Julien in Marseilles.

13. Marsatac Connexion Festival Hip-hop, June 2–3, 2000, at the Docks des Suds in Marseilles.

14. "Poulet" (Chicken) is a pejorative word for "cop" (translator's note).

15. A kind of family gathering of Marseilles's rap scene: about twenty groups followed one another (some very popular, others just starting out) before an audience of nearly ten thousand people (February 14, 2000, at the Dome in Marseilles).

WORKS CITED

Arendt, Hannah. *Between Past and Future*. Trans. Denver Lindley. New York: The Viking P, 1961.

Boltanski, Luc, and Laurent Thévenot. *Les économies de la grandeur*. Cahiers du centre d'étude de l'emploi 31. Paris: PUF, 1987.

Cheyronnaud, Jacques. "'La grand-messe du cinéma mondial.' Contribution à une approche socio-ethnographique du festival de Cannes." In *Aux marche du palais. Le Festival de Cannes sous le regard des sciences sociales*. Ed. Emmanuel Ethis. Paris: La documentation française, 2001. 29–52.

———. "La raillerie, forme élémentaire de la critique." *Critique et affaire de blasphème au siècle des Lumières*. Eds. J. Cheyronnaud, E. Claverie, D. Laborde, and P. Roussin. Paris: Honoré Champion, 1998. 73–128.

Groove. Special issue, hip-hop français 1 (1996): 24–30.

Le Professionnel. Dir. Georges Lautner. Original Soundtrack by Ennio Morricone. Cerito Films, 1981.

Masi, Bruno. "Apprentis rap à Marseille (Espoirs et système D: Le Festival Marsatac s'est fait l'écho de la jeune scène hip hop)." *Libération* 5 Jun. 2000: 33–34.

Mérit, Marius. Personal Interview. Direction Générale des Affaires Culturelles de la ville de Marseille, France. 5 Jun. 2000.

Pecqueux, Anthony. *Le Rap public: à l'épreuve sérieuse des institutions et nonchalante de ses publics. Contribution à une socio-anthropologie du rap.*

D.E.A. Thesis. Ecole des Hautes Etudes en Science Sociales de Marseille, 2000.

Searle, John R. *Expression and Meaning: Studies in the Theory of Speech Acts.* New York: Cambridge UP, 1979.

DISCOGRAPHY

Akhenaton (with Fonky Family). "Bad boys de Marseille—version sauvage." *Cut Killer présente hip-hop soul party III.* H-H productions/MCA, 1996.

———. "Bad boys de Marseille." *Métèque et mat.* Delabel, 1995.

Akhenaton, Freeman, and Le Rat Luciano (F.F.). "Le mégotrip." *Compilation Chroniques de Mars.* Kif Kif productions/BMG, 1998.

Busta Flex. *Sexe, violence, rap et flouze.* WEA, 2000.

D.J. Kheops. *Sad Hill.* Delabel, 1997.

Faf Larage. "Le fainéant." in D.J. Kheops. *Sad Hill.* Delabel, 1997.

La Fonky Family. "Sans titre." *Hors série volume 1.* S.m.a.l.l., 1999.

———. "La vie de rêve." *Soundtrack for the Motion Picture* Taxi. S.m.a.l.l., 1998.

———. *Si Dieu vent.* S.m.a.l.l.; 1998.

IAM. "L'école du micro d'argent." *L'école du micro d'argent.* Delabel, 1997.

Mos Def. "Fear not of a man." *Black on both sides.* Rawkus, 1999.

Suprême NTM. *N.T.M.* Epic, 1998.

Stomy Bugsy. "Le playboy de Sarcelles." in D.J. Kheops. *Sad Hill.* Delabel, 1997.

4

"Why Are We Waiting to Start the Fire?": French Gangsta Rap and the Critique of State Capitalism

Paul A. Silverstein

THE NTM AFFAIR

July 14th, Bastille Day, a day annually reserved for celebrations of France's liberal rationalist doctrine of liberty, equality, and fraternity, took on a new, ironic meaning when a 1995 *Concert des Libertés* (Freedom Concert) in the southern town of La Seyne-sur-Mer became the centerpiece of a set of legal and political controversies known as *L'affaire NTM* (The NTM Affair). Organized to protest the recent mayoral victory of the ultra-nationalist political party, the Front National (FN), in the neighboring Provençal cities of Toulon and Orange, the concert has become a symbol not of free speech and equality of political participation, as it had been intended, but rather of the inherent inequality within the French economic, political, and judicial system. A year after the concert, two rappers, Kool Shen and Joey Starr, from the suburban Paris-based rap group, Suprême NTM, were found guilty of "orally abusing" the security forces present while introducing their song "Police" during their performance.

At the time of the trial, the prosecution entered the song's lyrics as evidence against the group. "Police," from the 1993 album *J'appuie sur la gâchette* (I Pull the Trigger),[1] involves a virulent critique of police brutality against *banlieusard* (suburban) and immigrant youth, deriding the police as a "veritable gang" composed of "often mentally retarded," "brainless ones," and containing a fantasy sequence in which a character, "Joey Joe"—possibly Joey Starr's alter ego?—tracks down cops in the subway.[2] In presenting the song, they encouraged the crowd to

45

direct "Nique la Police!" (F**k the Police!) at the security guards present at the concert. They also encouraged the crowd to yell "Nique Joey
Starr!" (F**k Joey Starr!). Indeed, the group's name, NTM, stands for
Nique Ta Mère (F**k Your Mother), a common insult among French
youth and particularly common in the lower-class suburbs (*banlieues*)
and housing projects (*cités*) in and around France's urban metropolises.
The court, enabled by a common law protecting public authorities from
verbal insults, issued the two rappers an unprecedented sentence of six
months in prison (including a minimum three months served), along
with a fine of 50,000 francs.[3] Moreover, it banned the group from any
"professional activity" (including recording or concert appearances) for
the entire period of the sentence.

   The irony of the arrest and verdict were by no means lost on the larger
French public, as the incident escalated into a full-scale, nation-wide "*affaire.*" Demonstrations and marches in sympathy with the condemned
group occurred throughout France during the ensuing months. While conservative political parties lauded the judge's courage in harshly sanction-
ing the group's actions, leftist labor unions, political parties, and antiracist organizations vehemently protested the court's decision as a return
to an *ancien régime* of censorship and "moral order." They particularly
condemned the "double standard" of the French justice system that failed
to convict on several prior occasions FN leader Jean-Marie Le Pen for
publicly preaching racial inequality and denying the Holocaust—similar
crimes under French law. Likewise, they failed to see why NTM should
be subject to such censorship while xenophobic skinhead punk rock
groups, like Fraction Hexagone, have openly preached similar violence
against the police (in addition to Zionists and "cosmopolitans") (Anonymous, 1996: 7; Davet). The government's response was necessarily ambivalent. While the three concerned Ministries of Justice, Culture, and Integration initially upheld the ruling's legality, they nonetheless openly
supported freedom of speech. When it was later publicly revealed that the
presiding judge, Claude Boulanger, was under internal investigation for
handing down unusually harsh sentences and for personally chasing
down and arresting violators of traffic ordinances, the government with-
drew its support and instructed the public prosecutor to appeal the verdict
himself. Indeed, NTM's defending attorney had already lodged an appeal.
On appeal, the verdict was reduced to a two-month suspended sentence,
but the 50,000 francs fine and six-month ban on public performances
were maintained.[4]

The scandal has greatly increased NTM's public image as "hardcore" rebels, as "heroes" of French hip-hop, and served momentarily to save them from accusations of having "sold out" so often levied against other successful French rap artists like MC Solaar and IAM (Cannon, 159). As an ironic result, the group has clearly benefited from the publicity, achieving air-play on non-rap stations and skyrocketing its recent albums to platinum sales. In the meantime, its financial success has brought increased media scrutiny, producing a series of subsequent mini-*affaires* primarily concerning Joey Starr's repeated acts of violence against women.

NTM's 1998 eponymous comeback album registers an aesthetically refined and sophisticated understanding of the cultural politics and economic repercussions of the *affaire*. It commences provocatively with a continuation of the introductory fantasy from "Police"—a mock conversation between two police officers fearing the arrival of NTM—and proceeds to flaunt the return of the group to productivity and financial success in the first song entitled "Back dans les bacs" (Back in the Bins). In a later song, "On est encore là" (We're Still Here), the group narrates the *affaire* in its own words, denouncing the racism of the High Audiovisual Council (CSA). After a mock journalist's report from outside the courthouse in Aix-en-Provence where NTM's fate is about to be decided, Kool Shen returns to rap the verdict of the group—and perhaps of French republicanism as a whole.

The crux of the scandal and its aftermath points to a profound ambivalence both in the French state's projects for integrating (or, perhaps, "civilizing") its immigrant, minority, and poorer populations, as well as in the popular cultural response to such attempts, notably in the ever-burgeoning "hip-hop culture."[5] While the state, in alliance with multinational corporations, has encouraged the expansion of neo-liberal economic policies of commercialism and consumerism throughout its internal peripheries, it has nonetheless sought to regulate and contain the discourse and practices engendered by such expansionism. The NTM Affair outlines exactly this contradictory space where a virulent anti-government critique encouraged, commodified, and marketed by record labels both dovetails with and counters state political economic interests.

Likewise, hip-hop formations themselves, while enunciating an explicit critique of both state interventionism and the global market, have directly benefited from both and, to be sure, simultaneously desire their end and their continuation. NTM's response to state censorship—which one could gloss as "you look bad and we make money"—dovetails with a generalized ambivalent attitude among French rap artists to commercialism as political critique. MC Solaar, the most successful commercial French hip-hop artist worldwide, has famously deformed "capitalist" into *caca-pipi-caca-pipitaliste* (shit-piss-shit-pisstalist) ("Matière grasse contre matière grise" [Fat Matter Vs. Grey Matter], 1991), and portrayed neo-liberalism as a "new Far West" where "credit cards replace Remingtons" ("Nouveau Western" [New Western], 1994). Likewise, Assassin, whose logo appears on T-shirts and hoodies sold throughout France, has likened international trade to drug trafficking ("Légal ou illégal" [Legal or Illegal], 1995), accused the International Monetary Fund and the World Bank of promoting a *Guerre Nord-Sud* (North-South War), and causing the death of hundreds of thousands of children through its structural adjustment policies ("Guerre Nord-Sud," 1995), and generally declared war on capitalist "Babylon" where a Porsche "motivates more love than a mother nursing her children" ("Shoota Babylone," 1995).

NTM has itself criticized money's tendency to "rot people" and the capitalist system's maintenance of global inequality, while at the same time embracing multinational commercialism, with a multi-record contract with Epic-Sony since 1991 and a concomitant sportswear deal with Adidas. In other words, French "gangsta rap,"[6] while utilizing the expressive styles—from gangwear (sports pants, hoodies, bandanas, baseball caps, chunk jewelry, etc.) to colloquial (if not vulgar) forms of address and gesturing—of "hatred"[7] for the "system," clearly also embraces the rapacious possibilities enabled by the neo-liberal mode of accumulation. In other words, neo-liberalism outlines a France rappers love to hate.

FRENCH NEO-LIBERALISM

But none of this is particularly new. Avant-garde artists, regardless of their style or era, have long stood accused of benefiting from the system they overtly reject. Hip-hop artists in particular are well known for their ambivalent disavowal of capitalism and avowal of consumerism (Kelley, 1997: 44–45; Quinn, 81–83; and Rose, 40–41).[8] However, the contradiction engendered by the rise of successful urban cultural forms criticizing the means of their own success is especially salient in contemporary France, as neo-liberal austerity policies of market deregulation and welfare system dismantling have simultaneously increased urban poverty (and hence urban critique and violence), and paved the way for the ongoing influx of multinational capital into economies largely vacated by the state.

In this sense, it is necessary to abandon the celebratory tenor adopted by many academic studies that tend to view hip-hop as a "cultural expression of resistance" (Cannon, 155), a "critique of capitalism" (Gilroy, 197–99), or a "'hidden' transcript" *à la* James Scott that "critiques and resists various aspects of social domination" (Rose, 100). Rather, I am suggesting that we need to approach French rap as one expressive genre within a set of "signifying practices" (Kristeva, 65–74; Kelley, 1996: 121)—including other hip-hop arts like graffiti and break dancing—that open up a discursive space for young *banlieusards*, while remaining itself structured and delimited by a set of socioeconomic and cultural ambivalences at the heart of French late-modernity.[9] Within this ambivalently structured space, French rappers engage in processes of self-commodification—what Robin D. G. Kelley, referring to Paul Willis, has called "symbolic work" or "play-labor" (Kelley, 1997: 46, 57)—thus creating opportunities for local, national, and transnational social mobility in an otherwise static postindustrial landscape.[10]

For, in recent years, France, like many other nation-states in both the "developed" and "developing" worlds, has been struggling with a set of socioeconomic challenges associated with the rush to globalization. As has been well studied, this macro-process has taken on a myriad of forms throughout the world, as late capitalism (like all of its previous manifestations) has been indigenized in each local cultural environment.[11] In the French case, the movement to European economic and monetary union has both opened the country to job and capital flight and necessitated (in the name of currency stabilization) a reduction of state expenditures that has meant the gradual dismantling of the public sector. Both factors have contributed to the creation of a postindustrial economy, with increasing levels of unemployment that have nationally reached 13 percent and up to triple that in the working class areas that previously relied on the manufacturing sector (Daoud, 75).

Indeed, these statistics are even more disheartening when broken down by "nationality," particularly among populations historically employed in factory work.[12] As of 1990, unemployment figures for

foreigners were twice that of the national average (INSEE, 19, quoted
in Hargreaves, 40). Based on a slightly earlier household survey,
Michèle Tribalat discovered that the unemployment rate for 21-year-
old men and women whose mothers were Algerian was 39% and 49%
respectively, or about three times that of the children of mothers with
French nationality (Tribalat, 165).[13] When such figures are crossed
with unemployment statistics from the housing projects, the results
can reach as high as 85% (Daoud, 75).

    While French *cités* and HLMs (public housing projects) tend to be in-
credibly multiethnic and multiracial, with "foreigners" rarely making
up a majority of the local population, racial and ethnic "minorities" are,
for a variety of historical and structural reasons, relatively over-repre-
sented in comparison to other urban areas.[14] Indeed, the HLMs, built for
the most part in the 1960s, were significantly financed through the sale
of apartments to manufacturing concerns, who utilized them to house
their workers, many of whom were immigrants. In the heyday of the
Trente Glorieuses economic boom, buses from Renault, Talbot, and
companies would shuttle workers from housing projects like Val-Fourré
in Mantes-la-Jolie (50 km outside of Paris) to the factories in question
(Boubekeur and Daoud, 22–23). Today, with many of the factories
closed or not hiring, the *cités* have been marked by significant physical
dilapidation and the flight of local commerce, creating an atmosphere of
depressed sterility and an experience of social exile and "distraught."[15]
The concomitant stigmatizing effects of such dilapidation and impover-
ishment have made residence in certain *cités* an impediment to being
hired for a job, thus reproducing the very conditions of unemployment
that inaugurated processes of marginalization and prejudice in the first
place (De Rudder, 1990: 13). For instance, one friend from Val-Fourré
informed me that he always uses his sister's address in Paris whenever
applying for a job.

    Given these structural conditions, it is not surprising, perhaps, that
French housing projects have developed a healthy informal economy—
including a series of gray-market institutions revolving around the drug
trade or the fencing of stolen consumer items—for the provision of employment as well as goods and services not otherwise available or af-
fordable.[16] Not surprisingly, perhaps, such alternative economic ventures have contributed to a certain amount of theft and violence (what
authorities often denounce as "delinquency") against local stores, apartments, and commercial rivals that has attracted an increased police

presence in the *cités*. Not surprisingly, perhaps, this police presence has
increased tensions with inhabitants, tensions that have occasionally escalated since the mid-1980s into full-scale incidents of violent popular
unrest—termed "riots" by the national media—particularly when young
residents have been forcefully arrested or even killed by security
forces.[17] Not surprisingly, perhaps, these clashes with police have primarily targeted those state and economic institutions (notably police
stations, shopping malls, and municipal centers) symbolically associated by residents with their "exclusion." Not surprisingly, perhaps, this
violence and property destruction, when portrayed by the media as "riots," has had the effect of further underwriting the negative stereotypes
of these areas and contributing to the infernal spiral of social marginalization and the racialization of their residents as "other" (Silverstein
1998: 24–45). Not surprisingly, perhaps, these same areas are the birthplace of French gangsta rap.

The government's response to this urban socioeconomic crisis—often
referred to as *fracture sociale* (social fracture)—has been twofold. On
the one hand, since the early 1980s it has unleashed a series of urban renewal plans—leading to the creation of a complex network of national
commissions, urbanization laws, educational priority zones (ZEPs), and
funding programs—designed to reintegrate the *cités* in question into the
larger national and global economic systems and transform their inhabitants into productive citizens. These plans reached perhaps their most
elaborated form in Gaullist Prime Minister Alain Juppé's 1995–1996
"Marshall Plan" (which included the "National Urban Integration Plan"
and the "Urban Revival Pact"), following up on President Jacques
Chirac's promise of a "Marshall Plan for the *banlieues*" during his April
1995 election campaign. With the goal of luring young residents from
the street economy into the formal economy, the plan originally delimited 546 "sensitive urban zones"[18] in which local associations would receive state subsidies to hire young residents to work in paid internships.
At the same time, the plans established twenty "enterprise zones" in especially "hot areas" throughout the country in order to provide tax in-
centives to encourage the return of commercial ventures scared away by
the rise in suburban violence. As such, like the original Marshall Plan designed to reconstruct war torn Europe, Juppé's plan depended on an in-
sertion of capital into de-capitalized areas, though this time, in a neo-
liberal twist, with local associations and multinational corporations acting as the prime agents of change.

On the other hand, the French government has responded to the "crisis" of the *cités* with increased police intervention, predicating urban renewal on social and political quiescence. Reacting to the growth of "lawless zones in which the law of the Republic is totally absent" (Anonymous, 1995), the 1995–1996 plans added 200 plain-clothes inspectors to the already expanded suburban security forces to "penetrate the milieus of delinquency" (Leclercq, 23). In 1999, Socialist Prime Minister Lionel Jospin took these surveillance measures one step further, mobilizing 13,000 additional riot police (CRS) and 17,000 military gendarmes to patrol these same "sensitive urban zones," and thus effectively completing the militarization of the French suburbs.[19]

In this sense, France's adoption of neo-liberal economic policies has been necessarily equivocal. Nearly every franc it has saved by "tightening the belt" on the public sector—and for which it has incurred severe electoral wrath, including the December 1995 month-long strike by public servants—has been redeployed into the forces of security. According to former Gaullist Minister of Integration Eric Raoult, over 12 billion francs have been reinvested into the various *banlieue* plans (Raoult, 1), and the *banlieue* Marshall Plan has meant, first and foremost, the "reinforcement of the presence of the State" (Nouchi, 8). In other words, rather than implying the retraction of government from the economic sphere, as neo-liberal ideologues would have us believe, the liberation of capital flows has actually required increased state intervention (Martin, 4).

GUERRILLA CAPITALISM

Such ambivalence of state protectionism and retraction has had the effect of largely underwriting the growth of rap in suburban France. In its projects of socioeconomic reconstruction, the state has entered into partnerships with a variety of multinational corporations (particularly sportswear firms like Nike, Adidas, and Puma) that have sponsored social programs (such as sports summer camps and annual soccer/basketball tournaments) and have thus entered directly into suburban economic spaces (Silverstein, 2000: 34). In a parallel measure, major record labels like Sony, BMG, and EMI-Virgin have increasingly penetrated the *cités* to search out local musical talent and get them under contract before one of their rivals. Both types of direct corporate action, in the absence of other mainstream economic opportunities, have had the effect of underlining music and sports as two prime avenues for young men—as both activities are clearly gendered masculine—to escape the street.

Likewise, as such processes of economic globalization have facilitated cultural exchanges across Europe, the Mediterranean, and the Atlantic (with hip-hop as a clear emblem of a transnational, corporate-sponsored minority youth culture), they have also engendered a backlash of French cultural protectionism. Linguistically, this has meant an increased legal surveillance (including the 1994 Toubon Law) of the French language against Americanisms, Arabisms, and a variety of word plays (such as *verlan*) that mark the everyday language of the *banlieues* and the base of rap discourse.[20] Musically, this has meant the establishment of a series of legal quotas (the 1994 Carignon Law) requiring a minimum of 40% of musical programming on radio stations to be in French, and 20% by contemporary artists. Nevertheless, the law, which went into effect on January 1, 1996, and was named after the Minister of Communication, Alain Carignon, excluded "communitarian" radio stations, like Beur-FM or Radio Latina, which represent particular immigrant communities. Interestingly, given the paucity of successful mainstream musical production by French artists, the latter law has encouraged the growth and commercialization of Francophone rap (S.D. and V. Mo, 27). Whereas during the late-1980s, rap was relegated to underground and independent Parisian radio stations like Radio Nova (Cannon, 157), today it dominates the French FM band, and has become the mainstay of mega-stations like Fun Radio, Skyrock, and NRJ, all previously organized along the Anglophone-dominated pop/contemporary rock format. In this sense, French gangsta rap groups like NTM, while clearly the anathema of French conservative political parties, have ironically benefited from their laws.

However, just as much as contemporary French rap artists have profited from both multinational commercialism and state protectionism, they have likewise sought to short circuit the system and capture its fruits more directly. While continuing to depend on the multinational record corporations for the manufacturing and distribution, they have largely taken over the production, management, and marketing ends themselves. The Marseilles-based group IAM has established its own record label, *Côté Obscur*, which has already produced gold albums for groups Le Troisiene Oeil and La Fonky Family. Likewise, NTM's Kool Shen and Joey Starr have each established their own production companies (*IV My People* and *BOSS*, respectively), which have not only underwritten the careers of younger artists (including Bustaflex and Zoxea), but have also tended to cross corporate lines—with *IV My People* allied with Warner, while NTM is under Sony. Further, the intermediaries (often rappers themselves) established by the corporate record labels to procure young artists have begun more and more to act as entrepreneur-agents, demanding such increased control and profit-sharing that mainstream producers are likening them to a "mafia" (Rigoulet). Moreover, French rappers have attempted to garner control of the marketing end of the recording business as well. Realizing that television and radio advertisements failed to reach their target consumers (primarily suburban youth), rap groups have adopted a number of "street marketing techniques," from massive leafleting to local appearances. These practices, like rap itself, tend to be transnationally organized, as French street-marketing concerns (like Double-H Productions, founded by DJ Cut Killer) have learned directly from American marketing firms like Wicked and III Trendz (Rigoulet).

Furthermore, they have produced a number of inexpensive fanzines, with Anglophone titles such as *Down with This*, *Get Busy*, and *Authentik*, which promote the associated artists and their dependent groups (Cannon, 159). As such, rather than taking a revolutionary stance against the commercial system, French rappers have sought to infiltrate it directly, becoming "guerilla capitalists" as it were. As IAM rapper Imhotep has remarked, "[Young rappers] are understanding younger and younger. They hear talk of money, and they want a piece of it. They want to profit from the system, screw it over. That's what motivates them" (Rigoulet).

LOCAL CITIZENSHIP

Hip-hop formations based on guerrilla capitalism have moreover underwritten particular practices of citizenship within France's suburban peripheries. On the one hand, as renewed participants in the commercial/consumer sphere, suburban rappers and their posses have in effect reaffirmed themselves as "global citizens" (Joseph, 8). In becoming unmediated interlocutors with multinational firms and active participants in the transnational circulations of commodities and styles, they have become full-fledged members of new spheres of cosmopolitanism that link musical publics worldwide (Appadurai, 1996: 64). With reciprocal musical and ideological exchanges between Gangstarr (U.S.) and MC Solaar (France), between Wu Tang Clan (U.S.) and IAM (France),[21] new spheres of political contribution and contestation have been forged that traverse official political borders.[22]

On the other hand, eschewing formal, national political structures, rappers have affirmed their commitment to local constituencies, to "their people" of the *cités* from which they emerged. Like hip-hop groups in the United States, French rap artists have been organized around "posses," groups of fellow residents of their housing projects who often serve the groups as managers, promoters, security guards, and back-up singers.[23] They invoke such locality in tags, album titles, and song lyrics that reference their particular "inner city" belonging. For example, NTM constantly references their native Saint-Denis, or the larger administrative unit of Seine-Saint-Denis—and its short-hand postal code 93—in song (e.g., "Seine-Saint-Denis Style" [1998]) as well as in the name of their posse and tag, "93 NTM." For Ministère Amer, the reference is Sarcelles, or "95200" (the name of their 1994 album). Crossover groups likewise explicitly reference their particular native localities in their oeuvre, including Zebda's "Toulouse" (1995), Alliance Ethnik's "Creil City" (1999), and Cheb Mami and K-Mel's "Parisien du Nord" (Northern Parisian) (1998).

This "ghettocentricity" (Kelley, 1996: 136) is further evidenced not only in the themes of French gangsta rap focusing on life on the streets (including realistic portrayals of violence and drug dealing), but also in the musical and linguistic tropes used in the songs. Indeed, the vocal style of the rapping (e.g., the "flow") mimics everyday speech by youth in the *cités* not only in word choice (i.e., the use of various slang expressions and syllabic inversions [*verlan*]), but also in rhythm, enunciation, and prosody that can denote very specific localities and origins. By changing their flow, rappers can even play particular characters of everyday *cité* life, from the hardcore "gangster" (e.g., NTM "Plus jamais ça" [Never This Again], 1995), to the just off-the-boat immigrant (e.g., Alliance Ethnik "Intro," 1999), to the bourgeois Frenchman (e.g., Zebda "Je crois que ça va pas être possible" [I Believe It Won't Be Possible], 1998), to the police officer (e.g., NTM "Police," 1993). Moreover, in utilizing samples from other expressive genres, such as the journalist's report in NTM's "On est encore là" (1998) described above, or

President Chirac's infamous 1991 "Noise and Smell" political speech (Zebda, "Le bruit et l'odeur" [Noise and Smell], 1995),[24] French rap groups effectively normalize the *argot* (slang) of the *cités* as unmarked in contrast to the contextually marked speech forms of mainstream France.

This re-spatialization of the hood as the center of the rap groups' cognitive maps and imagined geographies entails particular political ramifications. The rappers' primary loyalty to these neighborhoods is manifest not only in the composition of their posses, but also in their dedications, credits, and acknowledgements that always "shout out" to their native *cités*. In addition, their treatment of inhabitants of the estate as "family"— a characteristic of everyday life in the housing estates where generational cohorts are called "brothers" and neighbors look out for each others' children (Duret, 27–62; Silverstein, 1998: 129–59)—emerges clearly in many French rap songs that invoke kinship ties to the song's imagined audience or referent, most notably in NTM's "That's My People" (1998). Assassin has taken this invocation of fictive kinship to its logical genealogical end, extending such local solidarity to political belonging and declaring their posse from the 18th *arrondissement* of Paris as their true "nation" (see "Kique ta merde" [Kick Your Shit], 1993).

Such expressions have frustrated French political parties from across the spectrum, who have hoped to instrumentalize the groups as mediators between the state and suburban residents, just as they did for an earlier generation of *Beur* cultural producers during the early 1980s.[25] However, whereas previous artists were attracted to the newly-elected Socialist Party's avowed diversity platform, the younger generation has been largely socialized in an atmosphere of continued economic inequality, structural racism, and police repression.[26] Government officials like Eric Raoult have reprimanded rap artists for not contributing economically and politically to their communities, for not being better role models and calling on their listeners to "fuck" racism, violence, and AIDS rather than simply the police (Roland-Levy, 7). Indeed, the discourse surrounding the NTM Affair was largely motivated by fears that NTM's incendiary lyrics against the "system" were actually responsible to some extent for recent street violence against police officers.[27]

French rap artists have generally denied a standard political role, either as role models or as potential revolutionary leaders: Kool Shen, in various songs, declares himself to be only a spokesperson, not a "leader" (see "Le Monde de Demain" [Tomorrow's World], 1991).[28] Joey Starr has expressed a similar position in interviews, claiming that "It's not up to me to explain what there is to do . . . We're just a reflection of what's happening . . . We don't throw stones at cops, only words. . . . Some people think we exaggerate; I'd say we tend to understate" (Herzberg and Inciyan). Contrastingly, MC Solaar, in spite of his "cool" flow has attempted to characterize this street journalism as "prose combat," alluding to his microphone as a "combat vest" ("La concubine de l'hémoglobine" [The Hemoglobin Concubine], 1994). Nevertheless, more self-described "hardcore" groups have criticized his indirect approach and artistic style, arguing for more frank and hands-on political tactics (Assassin, "L'entrechoque des antidotes" [The Knocking of the Antidotes], 1995).

On the one hand, Assassin has repeatedly claimed for itself the role of a vanguard revolutionary intelligentsia, posing on album covers with copies of Marx's *Civil War in France* and boasting that "We don't play with fire, we are fire, and the social politics of successive governments have provided the matches" (Blanchet, 31).[29] On the other hand, equally committed rappers like Hamé from La Rumeur have bemoaned the loss of rap's liberatory potential in its commercialism. In the end, most gangsta rap groups seem to have accepted their limited role in transformational politics as merely chroniclers of *la haine* (hate). For rapper Fabe and others, this has led to a particular political nihilism: "I don't reject the system. I'm in it, I can't kid myself" (Dufresne).

Most importantly, such attitudes point to the ways in which the structural conditions engendered by globalization have produced a generalized sentiment of political powerlessness. As Marxist critics Roger Burbach, Orlando Núñez, and Boris Kagarlitsky have argued, "Throughout the world, neo-liberalism has generated a palpable feeling that participation in any movement or protest is futile. Voting does no good, since one set of politicians is the same as another" (144). Joey Starr echoes this evaluation nearly word for word: "For people like me, a government of the Left or the Right is the same" (Dufresne).

Yet, this apathy with regards to formal or revolutionary politics should not necessarily imply the complete de-politicization of the suburbs. Rather, as I have indicated above, rap's production and consumption marks out a space of expressive politics that opposes the nation-state through both a prioritization of the local and an instrumentalization of the global, a space that I have elsewhere called the "trans-political" (Silverstein, 1998). While Joey Starr may have the impression that voting is like "pissing in a violin case," he nonetheless has a clear sense of his duties as a citizen: "Without going to vote, I am more of a citizen than most people. I do my civic duty in talking about what's going on around me, in keeping up-to-date and also being an outlet for some. I fulfill my obligations as a citizen every day, in writing my raps" (Dufresne). His political role remains to outline accurately the structural conditions of his locality (to represent his "people") and relate it to the larger conditions of inequality and racism elsewhere, to the global "monetary distribution" (NTM "L'argent pourrit les gens" [Money Rots People], 1991). In "Police" (1993), the song behind the *affaire*, NTM refers to Seine-St-Denis as "Chicago *bis*" (Chicago Two).

Furthermore, while adamantly denying any leadership or role-model capacity, NTM's latest album nonetheless has a pedagogical quality, with songs instructing parents to "not let their kids wander" ("Laisse pas trainer ton fils" [Do Not Let Your Son Wander], 1998) and "bad boys" to "put down their guns" ("Pose ton gun" [Put Your Gun Down], 1998). As such, if French rap has removed itself from the formal political arena, it has nonetheless outlined a sphere of local engagement and representational citizenship.

CONCLUSION: WHY ARE WE WAITING TO START THE FIRE?

The cultural politics of contemporary France, in all of its structural ambivalences and ironies, points to the poverty of the equally economic assumptions of neo-liberal ideologues and their critics. Dependency theory and other late-Marxist variants counter neo-liberalism's naïve assumptions about the future health of the capitalist system with an equally unquestioned faith in its imminent collapse (Amin). Whereas global capitalism's hero is the unbridled marketeer-consumer, its detractors' agent of revolutionary transformation remains the marginalized proletarian. What remains clear from the discussion above, however, is not only, as Marshall Sahlins has insisted, that global capitalism only exists insofar as it is indigenized in each locality (and therefore claims to it as a unified system only underwrite its ideological authority), but that the avatars of both globalization and its discontents are often one and the same.

Within this context, French gangsta rap artists exist ambivalently within a capitalist system they despise yet on which they depend for both the distribution of their message and for their financial well being, for their ability to escape the *cité* physically while still remaining attached to it ideologically. Enabled by the French state's economic abandonment of French housing projects to the marketing interests of multinational capital, rappers draw on their local embededness to articulate a virulent critique of the state policing apparatus and cultural politics of marginalization that continues to underwrite these very neo-liberal policies. While disengaging from formal (or even revolutionary) politics, they nonetheless retain a "hardcore" ideological bent that is more than merely stylistic or commercial. Indeed, if NTM's primary political engagement has been to express rather than incite violence,[30] they continue to avow the possibility of violent action as a necessary, if perhaps drastic means: "But why are we waiting to start the fire?" they asked in 1995 ("Qu'est-ce qu'on attend" [What Are We Waiting For?], 1995). "Just to be a few more in number," they responded after the *affaire* ("Odeurs de soufre" [Sulphur Smells], 1998).

NOTES

1. All translations are mine.
2. Fantasy sequences of cop killing in French gangsta rap are not particularly uncommon. See Assassin, "L'état assassine" (The State Murders), 1995; Ministère Amer, "Sacrifice de poulets" (Cops' Sacrifice), 1995.
3. Approximately $6,840.00
4. NTM had previously been the target of state censorship as well. The song "Police" had already been sanctioned by the High Audiovisual Council (*Conseil supérieur de l'audiovisuel* or CSA) from radio and television air-play. Likewise, at the insistence of the local FN Mayor and Prefect, the group's appearance in the June 1996 Chateauvallon musical festival in Toulon was cancelled. For a full discussion of the *affaire*, see Véronique Hélénon. The case against NTM is reminiscent of several rap-related controversies in the United States, particularly around the 1988 NWA rap "— — the Police" and the 1992 Ice-T/Body Count's speed metal fantasy, "Cop Killer." In the former case, the FBI encouraged police forces and promoters to block NWA's concert venues, and when the group did perform the song during a Detroit concert, the police on-site rushed the stage (Marsh and Pollack, 33–37). In the latter case, a letter signed by sixty congressmen denouncing the song forced Warner Brothers to recall the album and remove the track in question (Rose, 183). However, with the exception of a 1990 obscenity charge brought against 2 Live Crew, none of these incidents has resulted in legal action against the artists.
5. France has been a bastion of break dancing and graffiti artistry since the mid-1980s. Indeed, break-dancing crews remained well organized and commercially successful in France long after they had lost their popular currency in the United States and their particular moves had been thoroughly incorporated into standard popular dance styles (Rose, 50). The revival of break dancing as

a genre in the late 1990s in the United States points to a reversal of transnational flows of popular culture. For good histories of French hip-hop, see Olivier Cachin, Véronique Hélénon, and Georges Lapassade and Philippe Rousselot. For the American case, see Steven Hager, Tricia Rose, and David Toop.

   6. Throughout the essay I will be using "gangsta rap" and "hardcore rap" interchangeably to reference a set of hip-hop artists—including, but not limited to NTM, IAM, Assassin, Ministère Amer, and Les Sages Poètes de la Rue—identifiable by their "hardcore" musical poetics (in particular their harshness of vocal flow and complex layering of samples used) and their "ghettocentricity" (i.e., their focus on themes of violence, drugs, and prosecution identified with the "street" [*la rue*] or the "projects" [*la téci*]) that distinguish them from the more laid-back flows and less politically charged lyrics of MC Solaar, Soon E-MC, or Ménélik, as well as from the crossover styles of Alliance Ethnik, FFF, or Raggasonic (which nonetheless may contain socio-political critiques). In deploying the term, I do not wish to insert French rap into U.S.-based distinctions between more thematically "violent" but sonically laid-back West Coast (in which gangsta rap is generally grouped) and more "politically conscious" East Coast genres particularly relevant during the early 1990s. (Indeed, these geographic-stylistic categories are themselves problematic, as Bronx-based rapper KRS One is considered by many to be the founder of gangsta rap; and as LA-based gangsta rap artist Ice Cube has produced an album (*AmeriKKKa's Most Wanted*, 1990) with Public Enemy, the epitome of East Coast "conscious" rap, and has himself adopted at various times the rhetoric of black nationalism.) While the French groups in question certainly draw on gangsta imagery, their explicit politics and range of samples (including jazz, soul, and "old school" U.S. hip-hop, in addition to funk) transcends the traditional characterization of the U.S. "gangsta rap" genre. For a discussion of gangsta rap poetics, see Robin D. G. Kelley (1996: 119–24). For an attempt to create a genre system for rap, see Adam Krims (46–92). Note that Krims, in a brief reference to French rap, places NTM in the category of "gangsta rap," but refers to Les Sages Poètes de la Rue and Assassin as examples of a "conscious" genre, and groups IAM with MC Solaar as a "commercially successful group"—as if commercial success is incompatible with the other genres (155). Laurent Mucchielli, on the other hand, differentiates merely between "hardcore" and "cool" rap (60). For my purposes, such categorical distinctions are purely heuristic and essentially meaningless in practice.

   7. "*Avoir la haine*" (having hatred) popularly denotes an attitude of being fed up with life in the *cités* and rejecting the institutions and authorities that symbolize inequality and marginalization.

   8. Paul Gilroy has argued that an emphasis on consumption and pleasure in Afrodiasporic music (soul, reggae, hip-hop) actually constitutes a critique of capitalism's prioritization of labor and thrift (199–211).

9. See Zygmunt Bauman and Maxim Silverman.

10. In drawing on Anglo-American cultural studies and critical race theory, I am by no means assuming a fungibility of the categories and experiences of race and post-coloniality, or an isomorphism of cultural expressions of marginality, across the British Channel or the Atlantic. Rather, I am interested in processes of globalization and cultural exchange that create structural similarities across distances and underwrite imaginations of transnational solidarity. That French gangsta rappers explicitly borrow styles, samples, and rhetoric from their American counterparts is undisputed; that the resultant product or its local meaning and functioning within French suburban space is commensurable to American rap remains to be demonstrated.

11. For a discussion of late capitalism, its cultural rhetorics, and its global reach, see Arjun Appadurai (1990), Roger Burbach et al., Ulf Hannerz, David Harvey, Fredric Jameson, and Saskia Sassen. For a critique of the imperialist logic implicit in Marxian approaches to global capitalism, see Marshall Sahlins.

12. Note that French surveying bodies officially do not keep data on ethnicity or race, so socioeconomic figures for variously hyphenated, "minority" French men and women can only be estimated.

13. As of 1990, North Africans constituted nearly 40% of the foreign population in France, with Algerians a significant majority among them (INSEE R6).

14. See Véronique De Rudder (1992), Guy Desplanques and Nicole Tabard, and Alec Hargreaves.

15. See François Dubet, and Dubet and Didier Lapeyronnie.

16. While many residents have procured employment in service sector jobs outside of the projects, the informal economy in many ways monopolizes the economic life of the *cités* proper. For ethnographic and statistical discussions of the economic organization of the French *banlieue*, see De Rudder (1992), Colette Petonnet, Paul Silverstein (1998), and Catherine Wihtol de Wenden and Zakya Daoud. For a discussion of the postindustrial socioeconomic context of the Bronx and Los Angeles, the rival American centers of hip-hop, see Kelley (1996), and Rose. For a stunning ethnographic study of the informal economy of one housing project, the Chicago Robert Taylor Homes, see Sudhir Venkatesh.

17. Such confrontations include fire-bombing attacks in the Cité de la Cayolle (Marseilles) in 1981, the 1981 "rodeos" (car chases and burnings) in Les Minguettes (Lyon), and the 1983 weeklong standoff in Venissieux (Lyon). Other clashes between youth and riot police (CRS) occurred in November 1990 in the Mas-du-Taureau housing project of Vaulx-en-Velin after the death of twenty-one-year-old resident Thomas Claudio in a motorcycle chase with police; in March 1991 in Sartrouville after the assassination of eighteen-year-old Djamel Chettouh by a Euromarché supermarket security guard; and in May 1991 in the Val-Fourré *cité* of Mantes-la-Jolie after the asphyxiation of eighteen-year-old

Aïssa Ihich, denied his asthma medicine while held in police custody. A similar dynamic of state flight followed by violent unrest has occurred in Buenos Aires, the so-called "Paris of South America" (Burbach et. al., 30).

18. These numbers would increase by the June 1996 re-presentation of the plan before the National Assembly, from twenty duty-free zones to thirty-five, and from 546 sensitive urban areas to 744 (Bernard and de Montvalon, 7).

19. For a similar discussion of how state investment has abetted *de facto* urban segregation in postindustrial Los Angeles, see Mike Davis (223–63).

20. The law # 94-665 of 4 August 1994, which declared the French language to be "a fundamental element of the personality and heritage of France," mandated the use of French language in the French public sphere, including in all public gatherings and audiovisual contexts (though was not applicable to the musical works themselves). The fifth article further specified that foreign words or expressions must be excluded when an appropriate French word or expression existed. What constitutes a "French word or expression" is officially determined by the *Académie Française*, and the law empowers a set of nongovernmental cultural-linguistic associations to initiate legal proceedings against individuals, institutions, or corporations they determine to be in violation. In 1996, two such associations brought the Georgia Institute of Technology— Lorraine campus to court for its Internet site rendered exclusively in English (the case was dismissed). The law, which has generated great controversy in France, was popularly referred to as the *loi Toubon*, after the Minister of Culture Jacques Toubon who had proposed it and who was later mocked for his troubles as "Monsieur Allgood" ("All Good" being the literal translation of "Tout Bon").

21. In the case of MC Solaar, his appearance on Gangsta rapper Guru's *Jazzmatazz* album (1993) largely confirmed his career and respect in France (i.e., he was considered "serious" on the basis of American recognition). His "cool" flow, complex internal rhyming, and sampling styles have had a reciprocal influence on the acid jazz (hip-hop-jazz crossover) movement in Britain and the United States. In the liner notes for Solaar's 1995 album, *Prose combat*, American rap DJ and former host of the *Yo MTV Raps*' cable video program, Fab 5 Freddy, characterizes hip-hop as a global "culture" tied to the "high pressure, fast urban environment," and credits MC Solaar as one of its world promoters.

22. This is not to say that the state has become in any way politically irrelevant, but only that it is no longer necessarily the only game in town, and that questions of "representation" are being decided outside as well as inside national borders (cf. Sassen, and Glick Schiller et al.).

23. In the U.S. case, posses better define the cultural producers than the rappers themselves, as in KRS-One's *Boogie Down Productions*, Public Enemy's *The Bomb Squad*, and Ice Cube's *The Lench Mob*. Avowals of locality include *Boogie Down Productions*' "South Bronx" (1987) and NWA's "Straight Outta

Compton" (1988). See Rose (10) for a discussion of the place of the 'hood in American rappers' self-presentation.

24. In this 20 June 1991 speech that should deservedly be classed alongside Enoch Powell's 1968 "River of Blood" address in the annals of racist discourse, Chirac called for a revision of the family reunification immigration policy on the basis that large (polygamous?) immigrant families, in addition to their "noise and odor" (*le bruit et l'odeur*), supposedly benefit from French welfare while not paying taxes (*Le Monde*).

25. See Saïd Bouamama et al., Adil Jazouli, and Silverstein (1997).

26. In the introduction to a programmatic report entitled "Plural France" (*La France au pluriel*), Socialist presidential candidate François Mitterrand called for unity in diversity as France's future (Parti Socialiste, 10). As President, he released huge funding for the construction of community cultural and social development associations in the HLMs and actively sought to train local "cultural mediators" to negotiate between these multiethnic neighborhoods and the French state (Bouamama et al., Jazouli).

27. See "Qu'est-ce qu'on attend" (What Are We Waiting For) (1995). Just prior to NTM's initial sentencing, a police officer was put into a coma when he was hit on the head with a cement block while attempting to arrest two youths in the Parisian suburb of Villeneuve-la-Garenne. Also, a second female police officer was assaulted and raped while returning to her home outside of Paris. Raoult referenced these incidents in his interview in *Le Monde*, directly linking the judge's verdict to their occurrence.

28. Kool Shen's assessment of his role dovetails with the "street journalism" label attributed to U.S. gangsta rap and Ice Cube's own self-portrayal: "We call ourselves underground street reporters. We just tell it how we see it, nothing more, nothing less" (Mills, 32, quoted in Kelley, 1996: 121).

29. Assassin is a member of Marxist filmmaker Jean-François Richet's *Cercle Rouge* cooperative and has appeared in his 1995 film, *L'état des lieux*, brandishing Kalashnikovs.

30. "We explain [to rioters], 'we won't get in trouble, and you're not going to solve anything; CRS troops are going to come, and for two weeks they're going to break your balls and detain everyone and you're going to keep on complaining. What will you have won in the end? Nothing! You'll just seem like a bunch of jerks and the entire mess will continue.'" (Interview in *Authentik*, 32).

WORKS CITED

Aidi, Hisham. "France's Suburban Ghettoes: Liberté, Egalité, Fraternité." 2000. www.africana.com/DailyArticles/index_20000308.htm. 17 July 2001.

Amin, Samir. *Spectres of Capitalism*. New York: Monthly Review P, 1998.

Anonymous. "Raoult et les mecs cool." *Authentik* 1 (1998): 62–66.

———. "On est encore là . . . Suprême NTM." *Authentik* 1 (1998): 30–36.

———. "'Brassens, Ferré, Perret pourraient-ils encore chanter?'" *Le Monde* 17–18 Nov. 1996: 7.

———. "La FASP réclame un plan sur les banlieues." *Le Monde* 7 Sept. 1995: n. pag.

Appadurai, Arjun. *Modernity at Large: Cultural Dimensions of Globalization*. Minneapolis: U of Minnesota P, 1996.

———. "Disjuncture and Difference in the Global Cultural Economy." *Public Culture* 2.2 (1990): 1–24.

Bauman, Zygmunt. *Modernity and Ambivalence*. Ithaca: Cornell UP, 1991.

Bernard, Philippe, and Jean-Baptiste de Montvalon. "Les députés examinent la création de zones franches dans les banlieues." *Le Monde* 19 Jun. 1996: 7.

Blanchet, Philippe. "Les radicaux du rap." Interview with Assassin. *L'Evénement du Jeudi* 13–19 Jul. 1995: 31.

Bouamama, Saïd, Mokhtar Djerdoubi, and Hadjila Sad Saoud. *Contribution à la mémoire des banlieues*. Paris: Editions du Volga, 1994.

Boubekeur, Ahmed, and Zakya Daoud. "Radiographie de la plus grande ZUP de France." In *Banlieues . . . intégration ou explosion?* Ed. Catherine Wihtol de Wenden and Zakya Daoud. Special edition of *Panoramiques* 2.12 (1993): 21–24.

Burbach, Roger, Orlando Núñez, and Boris Kagarlitsky. *Globalization and Its Discontents*. London: Pluto P, 1997.

Cachin, Olivier. *L'offensive rap*. Paris: Gallimard, 1996.

Cannon, Steven. "Paname City Rapping: B-Boys in the *Banlieues* and Beyond." In *Post-Colonial Cultures in France*. Eds. Alec G. Hargreaves and Mark McKinney. London: Routledge, 1997. 150–66.

Daoud, Zakya. "Le chomage?" In *Banlieues . . . intégration ou explosion?* Ed. Catherine Wihtol de Wenden and Zakya Daoud. Special edition of *Panoramiques* 2.12 (1993): 72–75.

Davet, Stéphane. "Angry Young Men Target Police Force." *Manchester Guardian Weekly* 1 Dec. 1996: n. pag.

Davis, Mike. *City of Quartz*. London: Verso, 1990.

De Rudder, Véronique. "Immigrant Housing and Integration in French Cities." In *Immigrants in Two Democracies: French and American Experience*. Eds. Donald L. Horowitz and Gérard Noiriel. New York: New York UP, 1992. 247–67.

———. "De Varsovie à Barbès." *Différences* (MRAP). Special edition (1990).

Desplanques, Guy, and Nicole Tabard. "La localisation de la population étrangère." *Economie et statistique* 242 (1991): 51–62.

Dubet, François. *La galère: jeunes en survie*. Paris: Seuil, 1987.

Dubet, François, and Didier Lapeyronnie. *Les quartiers d'exil*. Paris: Seuil, 1992.

Dufresne, David. "Rap et Politique. Rendez-vous manqués.'Les rappers sont plus chroniqueurs que militants.'" Dossier Puissance Rap. *Libération* 26 Jan. 1999: www.liberation.fr/rap99/art6.html (no longer accessible).

Duret, Pascal. *Anthropologie de la fraternité dans les cités*. Paris: PUF, 1996.

Gilroy, Paul. *'There Ain't No Black in the Union Jack.': The Cultural Politics of Race and Nation*. Chicago: U of Chicago P, 1991.

Glick Schiller, Nina, Linda Basch, and Cristina Szanton-Blanc. *Nations Unbound: Transnational Projects, Postcolonial Predicaments, and Deterritorialized Nation-States*. Langhorne, Pa.: Gordon and Breach, 1994.

Hager, Steven. *Hip Hop: The Illustrated History of Breakdancing, Rap Music and Graffiti*. New York: St. Martin's P, 1984.

Hannerz, Ulf. "The World in Creolization." *Africa* 57.4 (1987): 546–59.

Hargreaves, Alec. *Immigration, 'Race,' and Ethnicity in Contemporary France*. London: Routledge, 1995.

Harvey, David. *The Condition of Postmodernity*. Cambridge: Blackwell, 1989.

Hebdige, Dick. *Subculture: The Meaning of Style*. London: Routledge, 1979.

Hélénon, Véronique. "Rap Music in the Land of Human Rights: The Prosecution of Supreme NTM." *Black Renaissance/Renaissance Noire* 1.3 (1998): 233–40.

Herzberg, Nathaniel, and Erich Inciyan. "Judge Jails Rappers for 'Verbal Attack.'" *Manchester Guardian Weekly*. Reprint of *Le Monde* 16 Nov. 1999: n. pag.

INSEE (Institut National de la Statistique et des Etudes Economiques). *Recensement de la population de 1990: Nationalités, résultats du sondage au quart*. Paris: INSEE, 1992.

Jameson, Fredric. *Postmodernism, or the Cultural Logic of Late Capitalism*. Durham: Duke UP, 1991.

Jazouli, Adil. *Les années banlieues*. Paris: Seuil, 1992.

Joseph, May. *Nomadic Identities: The Performance of Citizenship*. Minneapolis: U of Minnesota P, 1999.

Kelley, Robin D. G. *Yo' Mama's Disfunktional! Fighting the Culture Wars in Urban America*. Boston: Beacon P, 1997.

———. "Kickin' Reality, Kickin' Ballistics: Gangsta Rap and Postindustrial Los Angeles." In *Droppin' Science: Critical Essays on Rap Music and Hip-Hop Culture*. Ed. William Eric Perkins. Philadelphia: Temple UP, 1996. 117–58.

Krims, Adam. *Rap Music and the Poetics of Identity*. Cambridge: Cambridge UP, 2000.

Kristeva, Julia. "Four Types of Signifying Practices." *Semiotext(e)* 1.1 (1974): 65–74.

Lapassade, Georges, and Philippe Rousselot. *Le rap, ou la fureur de dire*. Paris: Loris Talmart, 1990.

Leclercq, Florent. "Banlieues: plan et arrière-plan." *L'Express* 9 Nov. 1995: 23.

Marsh, Dave, and Phyllis Pollack. "Wanted for Attitude." *Village Voice* 10 Oct. 1989: 33–37.

Martin, Randy. "Globalization? The Dependencies of a Question." *Social Text* 17.3 (1999): 1–14.

Marx, Karl. *The Civil War in France*. Peking: Foreign Languages P, 1970.

Mills, David. "The Gangsta Rapper: Violent Hero or Negative Role Model?" *The Source* Dec. 1990: 32.

Le Monde 21 Jun. 1991: n. pag.

Mucchielli, Laurent. "Le rap, tentative d'expression politique et de mobilisation collective des jeunes des quartiers relégués." *Mouvements, Sociétés, Politique et Culture* Mar.-Apr. 1999: 60–66.

Nouchi, Franck. "En attendant le plan Marshall sur les banlieues." *Le Monde* 28 Oct. 1995: 8.

Parti Socialiste. *La France au pluriel*. Paris: Editions Entente, 1981.

Petonnet, Colette. *Ethnologie des banlieues*. Paris: Galilée, 1982.

Quinn, Michael. "'Never Shoulda Been Let Out the Penitentiary:' Gangsta Rap and the Struggle over Racial Identity." *Cultural Critique* 31 (1996): 65–89.

Richet, Jean-François, dir. *L'état des lieux*. 1995.

Rigoulet, Laurent. "Business. A qui profite la rime?" Dossier Puissance Rap. *Libération* 26 Jan. 1999: www.liberatoni.fr/rap99/art5.html (no longer accessible).

Roland-Levy, Fabien. "'Je suggère à NTM de 'niquer' le racisme plutôt que la police.'" Interview with Eric Raoult. *Le Monde* 17–18 Nov. 1999: 7.

Rose, Tricia. *Black Noise: Rap Music and Black Culture in Contemporary America*. Hanover: Wesleyan UP, 1994.

Sahlins, Marshall. "Cosmologies of Capitalism: The Trans-Pacific Sector of the 'World System.'" *Proceedings of the British Academy* 74 (1988): 1–51.

Sassen, Saskia. *Globalization and Its Discontents*. New York: New Press, 1998.

Scott, James. *Domination and the Arts of Resistance: Hidden Transcripts*. New Haven: Yale UP, 1990.

S. D. and V. Mo. "Les réseaux FM protestent contre les quotas de chansons francophones." *Le Monde* 10 Jan. 1996: 27.

Silverman, Maxim. *Deconstructing the Nation: Immigration, Racism, and Citizenship in Modern France*. London: Routledge, 1992.

Silverstein, Paul A. "Sporting Faith: Islam, Soccer and the French Nation-State." *Social Text* 65 (2000): 25–53.

———. "Trans-Politics: Islam, Berberity and the French Nation-State." Diss. U of Chicago, 1998.

————. "French Alterity: Articulating Intra-National Difference in the New Europe." *Replika: Hungarian Social Science Quarterly* Special Issue (1997): 13–35.

Talha, Larbi. *Le salariat immigré devant la crise.* Paris: Editions du CNRS, 1989.

Toop, David. *The Rap Attack: African Jive to New York Hip-Hop.* London: South End P, 1984.

Tribalat, Michèle. *Cent ans d'immigration: Etrangers d'hier, Français d'aujourd'hui.* Paris: PUF/INED, 1991.

Venkatesh, Sudhir. *American Project: The Rise and Fall of a Modern Ghetto.* Cambridge: Harvard UP, 2000.

Wihtol de Wenden, Catherine, and Zakya Daoud. *Banlieues . . . intégration ou explosion?* Special edition of *Panoramiques* 2.12 (1993): 72–75.

Willis, Paul. *Common Culture: Symbolic Work at Play in the Everyday Cultures of the Young.* Boulder, Co.: Westview P, 1990.

Yo MTV Raps. MTV [Music Television]. Narrs. Doctor Dre, Fab Five Freddy, and Ed Lover. Produced by Jac Benson and Ted Demme. 1988–1995.

DISCOGRAPHY

Alliance Ethnik. *Fat Comeback.* Delabel, 1999.

Assassin. *L'homocide volontaire.* Delabel, 1995.

————. *Le futur que nous réserve-t-il?* 2 vols. Assassin Productions-Delabel, 1992.

Body Count (Ice-T). *Body Count.* Wea/Warner Brothers, 1992.

Boogie Down Productions. *Criminal Minded.* Jive, 1987.

Cheb Mami and K-Mel. *Parisien du Nord.* Virgin France, 1998.

Guru. *Jazzmatazz.* Chrysalis, 1993.

La Haine (Hate). Original Soundtrack. Perfs. Ministère Amer, IAM, La Cliqua, and Les Sages poètes de la rue. Delabel, 1995.

Ice Cube. *AmeriKKKa's Most Wanted.* Profile, 1990.

MC Solaar. *Prose combat.* Polydor, 1994.

————. *Qui sème le vent récolte le tempo.* Polydor, 1991.

Ministère Amer. *95200.* Hostile/Delabel, 1994.

NWA. *Straight Outta Compton.* Priority, 1989.

Suprême NTM. *Suprême NTM.* Sony/Epic, 1998.

————. *Paris sous les bombes.* Sony/Epic, 1995.

————. *1993 . . . J'appuie sur la gâchette.* Sony/Epic, 1993.

————. *Authentik.* Sony/Epic, 1991.

Zebda. *Essence ordinaire.* Barclay, 1998.

————. *Le bruit et l'odeur.* Barclay, 1995.

5

Rap and the Combinational Logics of Rogues[1]

Manuel Boucher
Translated from the French by Paul Rogers

As I have shown in a previous research project[2] regarding the protagonists of integration, the combination of logics (strategic, repressive, mediating, integrative, subjective) expressed by these actors reveals the face of a society riddled by rapports of domination and exclusion. Now, the weakening of this social link engenders a feeling of fear. Thus, in the big cities and more specifically in the peripheral popular suburbs, the representatives of the political authority and the actors of integrated society are worried, faced with the development of preoccupying phenomena for social cohesion. Faced with violence in schools, scholastic failure, car burnings in the peripheral sections of the towns, and the multiplication of uncivil acts (provocations, degradations, etc.), a fear of those immigrant and lower class youths is rising. One whole part of the multicolor and urban youth is becoming the symbol of the development of a new "dangerous class."[3] Consequently, the media and certain sociologists are developing phantasmic images of an unpredictable, uncontrollable, and violent youth rejecting the republican values of a "universal France" and creating its own subculture. In this pusillanimous climate, the advent[4] of hip-hop is often amalgamated with two stereotyped images. Indeed, hip-hop culture is associated either with demands consisting of violent behavior on the part of cosmopolitan youth influenced by the imagery of American ghettos, or with the expression of an esthetically postmodern culture. However, in France, since hip-hop culture got started in the 1980s, it cannot be confused with these two caricatures. Hip-hop is a polymorphous cultural movement, rich in its ability to teach us how a part of the multicultural youth originating in our occidental urban societies is trying to impose itself in the public space, while at the same time attempting to define itself as an actor-subject.

As a result, by basing my study on the research concerning the sociology of action I will show here that rap, an unavoidable form of hip-hop culture,[5] besides being the object of multiple stakes, (social, cultural, political, commercial), represents a mode of expression that combines both action and tension logic. In the transition between an industrial and a postindustrial society, the unified social world has exploded; it no longer has a center. In this context, one can only understand hip-hop culture if one seeks to close in on its expression, by situating it in the heart of a heterogeneous society. It is a society in which the actors try to give sense to their actions and to develop some sort of balance. From this point of view, the notions of social experience, as defined by François Dubet (91–134), or ethnicity, as defined by Michel Wieviorka (97–156) analytical continuations of *Tourainien* thought,[6] seem to be significant for comprehending these stakes and the meanings of rap in France. Indeed, the behavior of the youths from the suburbs, like that of the B-Boys,[7] reveals a certain amount of dispersion, "they live in several worlds at the same time, in 'communities' and in a culture of the masses, in economic exclusion and in a society of consumption, in racism as well as in political participation . . ." (Dubet, 18). There is a diversity of action logics (integration, strategy, subjectivity). The hip-hop experience concretizes itself at the point where the "classic" society is no longer a social reality, when the actors must manage several logics in a fragmented system.

INTEGRATION OR NORMATIVE LOGIC

Hip-hop is an idealized "limited" community around which part of contemporary youth, both urban and multiethnic in nature can identify itself, protest, contest, propose, act, and create. For these youths, the "hip-hop community" allows them to leave the anonymity of a mass society, while at the same time finding a place for themselves within it. This community also helps them to construct a cultural space that facilitates the recognition of self by oneself, but also the recognition of self by one's peers as well as by the society and its different representatives, in other words, by the world of the adults.

Hip-hop, at the heart of a multi-form society and without a clearly visible social unity, essentially seeks to construct normative orientations for actions, combining the values of a global society in which these youths would like to be integrated and recognized with those values belonging to micro-societies. The action, the demands of the rogues, is part of a quest for recognition and dignity for themselves and for the micro-society in which they feel they belong. In a quest for landmarks, for dignity, and for recognition, the rogues act in a framework combining the normative orientations of the action associated with the society, with those produced by the limited, very often symbolic community in which they define themselves.

The hip-hop movement functions enormously in a relation between Them/Us, which reinforces a feeling of belonging to a group and forges an affirmed identity. Thus, the conflict the rogues have with the system, the police, the business world, and showbiz consolidates their links of belonging to a group (the hip-hop movement, the youth of the suburbs, of particular quarters, of youths coming from immigration, blacks). In the same way, when the B-Boys define themselves as being part of a *posse*,[8] they establish a distance between themselves and other groups that structures them. The affirmation of visible differences, whether conflicting in nature or not, facilitates the constitution of a strong identity among hip-hoppers. The experienced, suffered, or demanded distance with the majority society fuses the feeling of identification and belonging of individuals within the hip-hop movement.

Finally, hip-hop appears as a cultural reaction, an attempt to construct modes of expression that give back a sense of dignity, of pride, and a framework for belonging to youths from diverse origins needing to affirm themselves, to demand, to oppose, and to build (within a movement, a posse, a form of expression such as rap, graffiti, or dancing) distinctive belonging and structuring links.

STRATEGIC OR CHESSBOARD LOGIC

Rogues act in a market-based society where the action logics are closely tied to the social rapports associated with a competitive system. For the B-Boys, to be member of a *crew*,[9] of a clan is part of a strategic logic. This allows them to affront the competitive world in which hip-hop is strongly invested. The posse, in which strong relations of solidarity exist, is a sort of carapace that allows them to advance in the market-based society. The hip-hop actors are completely invested in the heart of a society of unconstrained competition. Moreover, they are conscious of the competitive social relations that exist in the movement. The rivalry relationships of self-interest are very real to them. Between the B-Boys, the rogues, the *home-boys*,[10] the posses, competitive relationships undeniably exist.

One must not confuse, however, competition and the feeling of a challenge that is entirely part of hip-hop culture. We can see that hip-hop is a space that allows the actors to confront one another, to ally themselves, to compete in order to attain first recognition, but also eventually prestige and consummation. . . . The importance of the challenge, the verbal jousting in the rap expression, particularly during the "free-style"[11] sessions, underlines the competitive rapports between the "adversaries." The others, the *homies* (friends) with whom one *tchatches*,[12] with whom one creates a rap moment, appear as partners, at the same time as they can be perceived as potential rivals. The relations one constructs with the other members of hip-hop are sometimes mutually supportive and participate in the construction of hip-hop's identification, at the same time as they inscribe themselves in an exchange and a market rapport. Ideally, hip-hop is defined by its actors as being strongly structured as opposed to society, which is unfair, racist, discriminatory, and perverted by money and lust for power. It is a question of being "authentic," "honest," close to the foundations of society, to the oppressed, the victims of racism, and far from the amoral world of systems and corrupted men.

In reality, the hip-hoppers describe the movement as a hazy, heterogeneous space, where people "trip one another up." The groups, the posses become adversaries attracted or manipulated by "dough," "cash," and "business." The B-Boys is this type of group: above all competitors in a difficult market, rather than the mutually supportive members of one movement. As a result, the posses pursue their own interests, abandoning the mystified ideas (a unified street movement) that characterize the hip-hop movement. When all is said and done, the competition allows the B-Boys to build up their own prestige, by placing themselves ever closer to the sources of power, to money, while at the same time giving the impression of never betraying the people at the bottom of the social structure, their own roots.

Thus, hip-hop is certainly not a unified movement, but rather a real and virtual space in which groups, the posses, ally themselves or enter into opposition with one another in order to occupy an important place in the business and prestige market. Hip-hop, a mutually supportive, fraternal, and unified movement is nothing but a dream, a myth. Nevertheless, it is the hoped-for image the B-Boys most often put forward when dealing with people outside the "movement." Indeed, idealized hip-hop has an obligation to be "underground," authentic, pure, and uncompromising towards the system. Nevertheless, the desire to keep a certain authenticity combines with the longing to accede to some sort of recognition and to escape from anonymity. It is a question of bringing a message to a large public, while at the same time earning money, the ultimate consecration in a consumer society. When all is said and done, the rogues reject the system of the powerful, the dominators, and the established order, but certainly not the money. The ambiguity is perpetual; it is a matter of doing everything strategically so as to place oneself in the best way possible on the market, without necessarily losing the link that ties you to the movement, in other words to your roots, to the street. Besides, the B-Boys who become successful grow into exemplary figures who show that dreams of glory are possible.

LOGIC OF DISTANCING AND OF STRUGGLE AGAINST ALIENATION

Subjective action logic is the critical activity of the actors who cannot only be reduced to normative and strategic logics. Rap undeniably permits the majority of rogues to construct their own part of subjectivity, in other words their consciousness of the world and of themselves inside of it. By means of creative ingenuity, the rogues are the actors who express the realization of the subject and the construction of their liberty, by denouncing various felt or experienced sufferings (racism, marginalization, fear over an uncertain future). The B-Boys act then in the name of youth that is thirsty for recognition and respect; they are struggling against humiliation. They are conscious of being ridiculed and scorned youths, and they draw on cultural creativity and on identifying recognition as the affirmation of differences and of similarities. They call out to the world culture of the dominated against the system run by the powerful. They perceive themselves as the youth that characterizes the changing society faced with the old world, the youth of a maladjusted and obsolete system, the operator of an unfair social structure.

Furthermore, within French hip-hop, the theme of alienation is omnipresent. Rappers have the desire to fight against a certain form of negation of the conscience. It is a question of resisting and building alternatives to alienation taken in its most general meaning (subservience of humans as a result of external constraints—economic, political, social—and which leads to dispossession of self, of one's faculties, of one's freedom). When they make a call to awareness and resistance when faced with the alienation of which they are victims, the rappers are awakeners of conscience. For the B-Boys, defending against the risks of alienation, education, knowledge, and reflection are solid ramparts that must be reinforced in order to escape a vicious cycle.

In conclusion, I would argue that rap is the expression of a disarticulated, erratic movement in which the actors jump from one pole to another or associate several non-hierarchized logics. Hip-hop is a heteroclite and paroxysmal movement. Nonetheless, the homeboys want to react and act on themselves and their environment. There is an effort to constitute an action, to live and orient change such as reconciling the economy and culture. Certain people try to elaborate a collective identity, but the social adversary is vague, undetermined, and despite several attempts, the battle remains non-theorized and non-politicized. It is above all a cultural awakening, an awareness faced with the crushing power of a system that imprisons the spirit. For instance, in the French town of Evreux, a rap group chose *Prisonnier* (PSR) (Prisoner) as a name. Moreover, to rap, to create, to define oneself within hip-hop facilitates the development of a capacity for action adapted to changes: the social is progressively replaced by the cultural. Hip-hop and affirmation shape the space of resistance, thereby constructing an anti-establishment identity. This culture is essentially agonistic. At first only a defensive movement, the B-Boys eventually become indignant and revolt against a society that generates exclusion, suffering, and frustration. They also rebel against a racist and unfair system. They take the offensive when they rap and convey their messages, as well as when they invent and build a cosmopolitan art form. Consequently, hip-hop enriches, enlivens, and generates conflict in the complexity of the world. Thus, despite the tensions that are inherent to it, hip-hop seems all the same to be an attempt to build a social movement, but it remains fragile and unstable because the principal actors lose themselves in strategic, individualistic, and community-oriented logics. Whatever this may be, in their attempt to define themselves as subjects, the rogues confirm that they have the willpower to be conscious actors and not only submissive consumers.

NOTES

1. "Rogue" (lascar) is a synonym for "galley slave," youth from the suburbs. In French vocabulary, it also designates a hip-hop member.

2. See Manuel Boucher, "Les acteurs de l'intégration et leurs logiques. Entre consensus et éclatement."

3. Christian Jelen's *La guerre des rues. La violence et les jeunes*, and the radio show *L'Esprit Public* presented by Philippe Mayer on France-Culture Radio on Sunday mornings express this climate of suspicion towards youth and most notably those youths coming from immigration, on the part of the representatives of a dominating and media-oriented society.

4. A culture originating in the street that stages several types of expression. There is a musical pole (rap and Dj-ing), a graphic pole (graffitis, tags, and frescoes), a choreographic pole (break-dance, free dance). This includes clothing, values, symbols, etc. When all is said and done, it is an urban, technological, and multicultural culture. In the United States, "hip" literally means "competition," "hip" being derived from "hep," which in "jive talk" means a last cry and "hop" means to dance.

5. In this essay, I use the word "hip-hop" as a synonym for rap. This designation reminds us that one can only think of rap in terms of a bigger cultural ensemble represented by all the diversity of hip-hop culture. In addition, the rappers themselves more often use the term hip-hop when they are referring to rap.

6. See Michel Wieviorka and François Dubet, eds., *Penser le sujet. Autour d'Alain Touraine.*

7. Early term of the hip-hop movement that designates first the dancer (breaker-boy) and not a "bad-boy." Later, this term came to designate any member of the hip-hop movement.

8. A term that signifies a grouping together of individuals, of friends around a concept, creative activities within the hip-hop movement.

9. Synonym for "posse."

10. This African American term is used to describe someone who comes from the same neighborhood. It is thus a friend. In the hip-hop movement, it describes an accomplice who is fascinated by rap, by a common experience. By extension, this also means a member of the hip-hop movement.

11. Improvisation of different rappers, a rapological meeting of the posse based on a musical theme played repeatedly.

12. Editor's note: The slang verb "*tchatcher*," although understood and used in the whole of France, is mainly associated with the southern population, and with the city of Marseilles in particular. According to Daniel Armogathe and Jean-Michel Kasbarian, it refers to the wordy volubility of the Marseilles people in general (215–16), and to the Marseilles rappers in particular.

WORKS CITED

Armogathe, Daniel, and Jean-Michel Kasbarian. *Dico Marseillais*. Marseilles: Jeanne Laffitte, 1998.

Boucher, Manuel. "Les acteurs de l'intégration et leurs logiques. Entre consensus et éclatement." *Migrations-Santé* 96/97 (1998): 13–32.

Dubet, François. *Sociologie de l'expérience*. Paris: Seuil, 1994.

L'Esprit Public. Narr. Philippe Meyer. France Culture Radio, Paris, France. Sundays 11 a.m.–12 p.m.

Jelen, Christian. *La guerre des rues. La violence et les jeunes*. Paris: Plon, 1999.

Wieviorka, Michel. *La démocratie à l'épreuve. Nationalisme, populisme, ethnicité*. Paris: La Découverte, 1993.

Wieviorka, Michel, and François Dubet, eds. *Penser le sujet. Autour d'Alain Touraine*. Colloque de Cerisy. Paris: Fayard, 1995.

6

Social Stakes and New Musical Styles: Rap Music and Hip-Hop Cultures

Anne-Marie Green
Translated from the French by Mary-Angela Willis

The media has heavily influenced emerging musical styles that appeal to youth culture. As a result, the readership that wishes to maintain a social order generally stresses that the latest music (rock, rap, techno) results in behavior that can only lead to generational conflicts. These conflicts are manifested between youth and adults, primarily parents. Other media insist that these new musical styles are symptomatic of a generation within social and geographical contexts (i.e., rap represents youth in urban centers). A presenter at France-Culture Radio reporting a rap concert in Avignon, France, in July 2000 defined rap as a musical style adopted by youth revolting to urban discontent. The media further confirms this perspective in magazines, local and national newspapers, and radio programs. Facing such evidence, a sociologist must investigate the cause of these conflicts. Specifically, the correlation between musical taste and the youth's social background must be tested. For the past several years, my research[1] has allowed me to substantiate that the barrier between youth and adults, and even within the youth culture, is influenced by different musical styles.

If it is agreed upon, as anthropologists have insisted, music is a language without meaning, it is unintelligible and untranslatable. The listener is free to attribute any meaning to the music. As a result, music brings pleasure to the listener both on a personal and interactive level (outside of daily routines) since music expresses one's urges, influences one's intuitions, and affects one's vital functions (Jankélévitch, 7). This outcome explains why, in relation to all other cultural and artistic expressions, music defined by its distinctive, progressive, and contempo-

76

rary style belongs to the world of mundane pleasures as well as provokes intense passionate reactions.

Indeed, the multiple interpretations, even when the music is accompanied by words, establish communication at the symbolic, sensory, and subconscious-affect levels, which incite sensory manifestations where both the conscious and unconscious participate: "It is a resonant awareness actuated by secondary psychological sensibilities which remain in the unconscious mind" (Michel, 163). Therefore, it is as difficult for youths as it is for the adults, who may be stigmatized and outcast, to discuss music, particularly in the presence of real or symbolic mediators. This confirms Vladimir Jankélévitch's remarks that music "is not intended to be discussed" and that "it is not intended to be said (. . .)," it "was not invented so one could talk about it" (Jankélévitch, 101). As such, one can confirm that this perspective is at the heart of current studies conducted on musical behavior as well as on its importance within social spheres. Characterizing these social spectrums are youths experiencing academic failure and inadequate language skills. Further investigation into the relationship between youths and rap music is warranted. However, this problem is not manifested solely among the creators of rap since it is their language skills that allow them to be defined as rappers.

Moreover, certain presuppositions and stereotypes lie within an old, deep-rooted, and significant tradition that attributes musicians—and artists in general—with characteristics of originality and marginality. This serves as a vehicle for new forms of music. It bestows music with respect that is rarely questioned. Musicians become symbols enriched with mythical qualities. Music's origin is therefore considered incomprehensible and its destiny unpredictable. It is surrounded with mystery and the musician's symbolic image—that of the "inspired," "gifted," "exceptional" creator—influences its social progression, reception, and assimilation. The musician's symbolic image goes on to embody musical genres rather than the music itself. As a result, the assimilation of the musician's life creates a more powerful impact on the general public than the musical genre itself. It is for this reason that emphasis is placed on the rap musicians' ethnic and geographic origins. For example, they are defined as becoming stars despite their urban origins.

The musician's unexpected and inexplicable talent dominates, whether in the act of composing or interpreting music. In other words, it is difficult to associate a musician's inspiration to an actual intent or destination. If meaning is perceived, it is unrelated to the actual art of creation. Such a conception of the musician and music is so deeply embedded in society's collective psyche it hinders interpretation; music's value cannot be carelessly quantified. Instead, it evolves from its power to incite an emotional reaction from its listeners who may also identify themselves with a particular musical style. In the history of music, trends and styles have been influenced by myths that steer the listener to focus on non-artistic characteristics. Thus symbolic figures are simplified and curtailed within a framework of the exchange of information in our contemporary society. As a result, music's influence is further enhanced by the musician's "mythological" persona as well as the musical style itself. A mythology of talent makes it impossible for both youth and adults to attempt an analysis and understanding of the different genres of music that appeal to the listeners (musicians and composers may well consider this an outrage). Music's popularity is influenced by the way the musician and his/her musical style is promoted; biographical anecdotes contribute greatly to this process. Consequently, the barriers between the two are reinforced and it is no longer simply a matter of rock, rap, or techno but more of a random musical style that contributes to it.

In general, the media tends to classify youths and their musical taste into large categories in which they often would rather not be associated. So, we find some youth who do not listen to classical music but who enjoy rock, rap, or techno. In turn, the opposite may be associated with adults who do not necessarily share the same musical taste as youths. The media does not attempt to explain why some fans have been loyal to the same rock musicians for forty years while those same musicians continue to acquire new fans of the younger generation. One can then conclude that today's rap fans will still be fans in the future. The study of rap and hip-hop is not limited to a discussion of music appreciated by youths. It is therefore interesting to pay close attention to and understand the myths that perpetuate social barriers between adults and youths from urban and impoverished neighborhoods.

My research has allowed me to question and to mitigate these presuppositions. Empirical research has shown that youth culture is influenced by their age and social origin. In addition, in modern Western society, belonging to particular geographical regions has consequences. For this reason, rather than pursue an argument that dichotomizes youths' and adults' behavior to music, I chose to research the relationship between youth and music and the impact music has on them.

The majority of studies that focus on the behavior of youth define adolescents in terms of age. That is why they are considered too hastily as a homogeneous group. Consequently, a new social category has emerged, that of youth, whose main characteristic is its state "of prolonged uncertainty which evades an effective social role and questions identity" (Galland, 72). Pierre Bourdieu describes them as socially "outcast" (1993: 96). Nevertheless, youth influence the economy to a great degree, particularly consumer products pertaining to pop culture and art. Therefore, an increase in art industries can be detected from the 1950s that began producing more socially acceptable products influenced by subversive musical trends. All musical trends have not escaped this tendency and nor has rap.

Similarly, a social community has evolved whose development encompasses social structures as well as methods of socialization. In addition, confining youth within this new social category is hampered due to the absence of explicit rules. The social transformation of modern society leads to a double movement of differentiation and integration. Gradually, as this social change develops, and as barriers between social classes and referents become more vague and uncertain, the process of differentiation takes hold. Thus, as society becomes more complex, a process of integration counterbalances the diverging effects of such differentiation. Therefore, the musical tastes of adolescents can be analyzed and understood through this process. That is why if rap first manifested itself within youths from urban "ghettos," it can therefore also encompass youths from every social background.

In *The Division of Labor in Society,* Emile Durkheim demonstrated that along with the division of labor reinforcing cooperation, the effects of alienation are reduced and one can therefore understand why new networks of communication appear in society, which favor the emergence of new ties between individuals whose interests tend to differ progressively. Talcott Parsons and his followers support this same theory. They highlight the emergence of more complex and diverse social subcultures akin to the discovery and invention of new activities, behavior, norms, sanctions, or gratification, which all play a role in the process of integration. In many regards, modern forms of music ranging from all forms of rock, rap, and techno play a vital role in the dialectic process of societal transformation.

In 1942, Parsons began studying social change through musical styles favored by the youths. He defined the system of alternatives and uncertainty that characterizes the youth cultures within industrial societies (Parsons, 89–103). In order to break through these social constraints, the youth develops subcultures and creates a "civilization of youths." This allows them to redefine themselves and to reduce a semblance of alienation by enhancing integration, and by creating spaces of acceptable deviance, which accomplish the task of regulating the social system. Parsons defines youth culture with notions of "romanticism" when problems of alienation are resolved. This hedonistic romanticism rejects traditional values of gratification of difference in favor of values, which reinforce the fusion of the group or community. Hyperconformism of musical trends and styles is at the center of juvenile sociability. This explains why the appreciation of music by a common group plays a key role. It is in this context that rap music must be studied and understood.

In the 1950s and 1960s, the central role that music played in the socialization process was often evoked in the emergence of a youth subculture on a broad level and the development of the *yé-yé* phenomenon in France on a specific level (Morin, 435–55). English writers at the time displayed a keen interest in the relationship of youth and music, and coined the term "taste cultures" to define this aspect of musical tendencies. They focused on complex social determining factors concerning esthetic judgment and refuted any correlation between social class membership and the appreciation of certain musical styles. According to their findings, musical preferences reflected a shift in group membership, unions, and associations between diverse individuals who transcended social class, age, and education. In fact, these findings converge with conclusions based on my empirical research.

The concept of taste culture highlights the division of large social categories into smaller groups characterized by the preference to different styles of music. These groups are defined as "taste cultures." This definition compensates for the insufficiencies and reductive aspects of a sociological theory that relies purely on demographic statistics or on the study of invariants and determinants according to ethnicity, social class, gender, education, and geography.

Moreover, certain authors emphasize that these groups are attracted to a particular musical style as much based on personal choice as on social opportunity since music is accessible to the masses. It is therefore evident that music put forward by the media is accessible to youth of underprivileged and immigrant sections of the population. In this respect, the lack of quality education and access to music broadcasting play an important role.

In addition, the majority of studies emphasize youths' strong adaptation to taste cultures, also referred to as "esthetic subcultures." These taste cultures depend on music listened to by groups whose constitution cannot be determined by specific factors other than a shared interest in the same music. Members of these groups are led to believe that their taste in music is purely personal and spontaneous. However, concerning music, the cultural identity of adolescents is manipulated and controlled by the media and cultural industries since they are the ones in control of its development and evolution. It is in this sense that a broader view must be adopted when studying preconceived ideas concerning rap (its purity, authenticity, independent labels, etc.).

Art plays a dominant role in cultural taste tendencies. In fact, as mentioned previously, formal and external criteria that determine different styles or different taste in music are very ambiguous. Nonetheless, the difficulty in defining these objective criteria stems from the fact that members of taste cultures are easily influenced by nuances that capture their eye.

Consequently, with the appearance of new interpreters, records, music genres, and media outlets, it is understandable that in the absence of explicit criteria, members of taste cultures develop formal and informal means of defining an esthetic consensus on the value of new musical trends. These new mediums are defined according to certain questions: Are they a part of the group's common heritage? Must they be rejected? In short, youths must determine if such a work is favorable. Most of the time each individual member of a taste culture does not make such decisions. Furthermore, the media attributes "good" reviews to the already "initiated" circle of artists and assigns well-argued and coherent esthetic judgment to the less experienced in order to guarantee respect to new musical forms, such as in the case with rap and hip-hop.

Current industrial societies elicit the creation of groups whose members share similar musical styles while simultaneously belonging to a different social status. A case in point is the error in associating rap music with youth from urban centers. The clearly defined taste culture is very closely linked to transformations within society. The more complex a society, the more its members will exhibit different reactions to music. This explains why sub-categories within rap emerge to provide different youth cultures a sense of appreciation and identification with a particular taste culture.

Yet, according to Max Weber's theory, taste cultures ascribe more to status groups than to social classes. Specifically, while social classes are defined based on their ability to acquire goods and services, status groups are defined depending on the acquisition of certain goods, such as cultural or artistic goods, including music. Therefore, consumerism is used to reaffirm social status and legitimacy. Taste cultures use an array of cultural accessories that serve as more than just pastimes, but as signs of distinction and differentiation. Owning the "right" T-shirt, listening to the "right" record, displaying the "right" poster in one's room, wearing the "right" athletic shoes, shopping in the "right" stores, going to the "right" clubs, and participating in the "right" raves are used by youths to assert their values and their styles, and even to attain a certain status. Consequently, the media plays an essential role in transmitting these symbols. A pattern of association predetermined by the arts industry is put into effect between adolescents and musical styles. This occurs even if, at first, a specific form of music does not intend to ascribe itself to particular cultural symbols. In fact, musical styles largely voice a protest against society and commercialism. Despite an attempt at disguising these voices of protest, the music industry nevertheless associates certain musical styles with disgruntled adolescents. To demonstrate this hypothesis on rap at this point would be too lengthy.

In Western society, groups of friends are created based on shared musical taste. At the center of these groups one finds leaders, or trendsetters, who represent the group before the media. Finally, this empirical data indicates that the youth, irrespective of their social class, pursue a sought-after style that can be assessed symbolically and concretely, but that is completely determined emotionally. The results also assert that one can only understand the behavior of youths by analyzing the variety of meanings associated with different musical styles as exhibited through the act of listening to music, playing music, and other expressions.

Concerning hip-hop, it is less a matter of determining the significance of belonging to the hip-hop culture, adhering to a rap movement, or understanding how the behavior of the youths is organized, than an understanding of how the game of cultural identity affects its acquisition. It would seem that a hip-hop cultural movement does not exist according to the usual objective criteria as a homogeneous group defined by comparison to other similar groups. Musicians and their entourage at the center of hip-hop culture differ considerably from each other, be it by their social origin, their educational background, or even their musical trajectory. Therefore, a statistical study that includes opinions and behavior is inadequate in understanding the collective dimensions that define group.

The growing popularity of the hip-hop movement is indicative of a division and, thus, of an ever expanding "heterogenization" separate from the movement. This quantitative and qualitative growth, due in part to the legitimization of rap,[2] and the fact that technical advancement is relatively slow, opens hip-hop culture to an array of new social influences. This is due to a blurring of social landmarks.

Whereas a strong hip-hop identity lies at the center of hip-hop culture, fewer characteristics are also found on the periphery. Paradoxically the unity of hip-hop culture is founded on the diversity of its members and their lifestyles. One hears that hip-hop is "full of social and musical meaning" (Lipianski, 35–42), which illustrates a worldly dimension superceding its identity as a collection of musical works. What is recognized today as "hip-hop" or "rap" is compared to a generic category of social behavior. Therefore, hip-hop culture assumes a social space that fulfills an important function in identity formation. Hip-hop is a "movement" that members adhere to both cognitively and behaviorally; it is a reference group in which culture and identity are closely linked.

It is evident that behavior associated with hip-hop culture depends on the projection of creative and artistic identification. These musical styles elicit support that unites a community's concerns known as a "culture of taste." Definitions of taste, and more precisely of "good" or "true" taste, are more easily acquired by youths than by the unexposed. Regardless, values within a community clearly appear that steer youths to share similar outlooks on life and on the future. Music effectively captures youth's attention. Whereas the youth's general sentiment of weariness and rejection concerning today's society (in particular politics and religion) predominates, music remains widely embraced, each musical style corresponding to a particular outlook on life.

Moreover, I have been able to assert that musical styles appreciated by the youth culture, along with the behavior associated with music, are capable of seducing as well as shocking adults. Nevertheless, youths who actively participate in particular musical lifestyles defend themselves clearly and lucidly whereas adults continue to surround such tendencies with an air of mystery and imagination. The behavior exhibited by rockers, rappers, and ravers is not always understood and may even illicit fear. Even though the virulence and transgression of the youth culture is limited to verbal expression, it very rarely translates into action. Popular behavior of groups seems to elude the adults' control, and for this same reason, such behavior can both seduce and scare. The behavior of youths towards music is a cultural phenomenon whose importance points to the youth's need for self-affirmation rather than a "product of false conscience" or as a "diversion to an otherwise banal existence" (Adorno, 11).

As a result, I affirm that today's modern music, in all its diversity, plays an explicit and vital role in the socialization of youth, regardless of social background, age, gender, or education (Elias, 29). As a matter of fact, the body of empirical evidence that I have gathered opposes hasty judgment on musical trends adopted by youths and their supposed conflicts with adults.

Before engaging in any argument one must keep in mind that, in terms of its conceptuality, music is open to interpretation and therefore youths are free to ascribe any meaning to it. Also, one must not forget that in our society, pleasure is viewed suspiciously since it is an aspect of an individual that society as a whole cannot control. This is why, for the benefit of society, it is preferable to both "massify" youths' musical tastes at the risk of creating a barrier with adults, and to allow for sociocultural mechanisms of self-determination, at the risk that the reproduction of a musical culture stays minimal. That is how their pleasures are channeled.

My studies show that the pleasure one acquires through music is ever present in the relationship between youths and music. Emphasis is also placed on the autonomy of musical language: it is a source for dreams and pleasure. This process of sublimation allows youths to perceive the outside world while practicing self-realization and experiencing an awakening of the imagination. In addition, youths are free to associate their own interpretation of the music, which can also reflect their state of mind. However, according to Albert Memmi,

> It's easy to see why pleasure has had a bad press. (Has anyone ever noticed that for each pleasure there is a corresponding sin?) It is a part of the

individual that eludes the group, which strives to completely control each of its members. Pleasure without social control risks running counter to society's goals. (77–78)

It must be accepted that rock, rap, and techno are today's musical trends of youths. At the same time, it is much more than just music; music represents multiple facets of a collective self-actualization. Furthermore, all of my research alludes to references of emotions and pleasure. Therefore, one may conclude that whatever social reasons may explain inclinations towards particular musical styles other factors may influence youths' tastes in music. In fact, in the face of youth culture's sense of "disenchantment" with the world, music provides them with an "escape," giving meaning to their lives. For this reason, it is impossible to view musical practices and behavior independently without considering their content and functions. Music that youths are drawn to is a cultural phenomenon. In conclusion, there is no difference between the appreciation of one type of music over another: its importance and youth culture's expectations remain constant. It would be inappropriate to view today's modern music solely on its power to sway the masses. Truly, these musical styles have been influenced by the passing of time. It is then necessary to view music as an expression of its time.

NOTES

1. See Anne-Marie Green, *Les adolescents et la musique*; *Les personnes âgées et la musique*; *Des jeunes et des musiques: Rock, Rap, Techno . . . ; Musique et sociologie: Enjeux méthodologiques et approches empiriques.*
2. See Pierre Bourdieu, *The Rules of Art.*

WORKS CITED

Adorno, Theodor. "Sociologie de la musique." *Musique en Jeu* 2 (1971): 11.
Bourdieu, Pierre. *The Rules of Art: Genesis and Structure of the Literary Field.*
1992. Trans. Susan Emanuel. Stanford: Stanford UP, 1996.
———. *Sociology in Question.* 1984. Trans. Richard Nice. London: Sage, 1993.
Durkheim, Emile. *The Division of Labor in Society.* 1893. Trans. George Simpson. New York: Free Press, 1964.

Elias, Norbert. *Sport et civilisation, La violence maîtrisée.* Paris: Fayard, 1980.

Galland, Olivier. *Les jeunes.* Paris: La Découverte, 1990.

Green, Anne-Marie. *Musique et sociologie: Enjeux méthodologiques et approches empiriques.* Paris: L'Harmattan, 2000.

———. *Des jeunes et des musiques: Rock, Rap, Techno . . .* Paris: L'Harmattan, 1997.

———. *Les personnes agées et la musique.* Issy-les-Moulineaux: Editions E.A.P., 1994.

———. *Les adolescents et la musique.* Issy-les-Moulineaux: Editions E.A.P., 1986.

Jankélévitch, Vladimir. *La Musique et l'Inéffable.* Paris: Seuil, 1983.

Lipianski, Edmond-Marc. "Communication interculturelle et modèles identitaires." In *Identités, cultures et territoires.* Ed. J.P. Saez. Paris: Desclée de Brouwer, 1995. 35–42.

Memmi, Albert. *Dependence: A Sketch for a Portrait of the Dependent.* 1979. Trans. Philip A. Facey. Boston: Beacon P, 1984.

Michel, André. *Psychanalyse et Musique.* Paris: PUF, 1951.

Morin, Edgar. "Adolescents en transition." *Revue Française de Sociologie* 7 (1966): 435–55.

Parsons, Talcott. *Essays in Sociological Theory.* Glencoe, Il: The Free P, 1954.

Weber, Max. *The Rational and Social Foundations of Music.* 1921. Trans. Don Martindale, Johannes Riedel, and Gertrude Neuwirth. Carbondale: Southern Illinois UP, 1958.

7

Tags and Murals in France: A City's Face or Natural Landscape?

Alain Milon
Translated from the French by Seth Whidden

Phenomena dating back to the mid-1980s, tags and murals seem to modify the City's face by integrating more or less successfully into the urban environment. Some people consider these marks to be dirt or visual pollution, while others see them as specifically urban expressions that fully participate in the life of the City. In reality, the question here is not to judge the value of these "marks," but rather to examine how they participate in the construction of this urban face or landscape. Are tags and murals a part of a city's skin, or are they but scars more or less deeply engraved on its body? To answer this question, it will be necessary to consider the singularity of these marks that lack their own proper space, tags, and murals.

THE NATURE OF TAGS

Those who do not understand them often consider tags to be incomprehensible hieroglyphic signatures that aggressively pollute the visual space of the inhabitant, a type of filth that damages the City's attractiveness. These marks are felt as dirty, exterior marks on the City. In other cases, they are perceived as integral parts of the City; they contribute to the definition of its exterior aspect, its size, as well as to the definition of its interior design, its soul. They are not simple decorations but also the translation of a social unrest.

But is the tag an incomprehensible mark, a scribble, a hieroglyphic sign, an imprint, a territorial marking, a logotypic signature, a painted piece of filth, or some new kind of fresco, or mural art? Perhaps all of the above. Let me simply state that the tagger plays with the strange feeling that these visual signatures provoke, which is not unproblematic if we understand these mural signatures to be expressions that shape the City's landscape. How are we to understand that these visual forms, while not belonging to the City, make up a part of the landscape that surrounds us? To avoid any misunderstanding, let me first define the tag and distinguish it from the graph, scribble, murals, stencils, mosaics, and shadows.

A tag is made up of several aspects. It is first and foremost a more or less complex monochromatic mural signature that is sprayed very quickly on a wall. Tags come in different varieties. They can be signatures on a small self-adhesive label, a sticker. This type of procedure has several advantages. Its author can, depending on his use of "torches" (large markers), pay close attention to the esthetic effect of his or her signature. In addition, sticking these labels to walls is very discreet and thus practically risk-free, and the quality of the materials guarantees a long life for the sticker. The "burn" is a mono- or multi-chromatic lettering that is more carefully and artistically written than the tag. It has several variations that come from the quality of the "border," of the spray on the wall and the kind of cap used. There is also "throw up," the simplest kind of burn, made with a maximum of two colors: one for the outline and one for the letter itself. The "block style" is a burn made up of block letters; "top to bottom" indicates, in the case of subway cars, that it covers the side of the car from top to bottom, whereas the "panel" refers to lettering that only covers the lower panel of a subway car. There are also several calligraphies for the lettering: the "bubble" or "flop" (letters round like balloons); the "drop" or "block style" (block letters completely covering a well-defined space); the "wild style" (stylized mix of various letters). The last and most evolved form of expression is the "fresco" or "mural," which must not be confused with stencils like those of Miss-Tic, Bleach, or Mesnager,[1] nor with shadow outlines (outlines of a sign or parking meter, often painted in white on the sidewalk), nor with "mosaics" (little mono- or multi-chromatic mosaics sealed on a wall or a sidewalk). Representing a slice of daily life in fluorescent colors on a support like a fence or a wall, the "mural" is a complex graphic work, letters, or drawing made from a sketch.

Often, letters and drawing are mixed, in which case they are referred to as a "fresco," a term that should be taken here to denote a scene from daily life. The "mural" or "air-sprayed fresco" is a decorative art like

MC Solaar *(Photo by Philippe Bordas, courtesy of Sentinel Ouest, © 2000)*

MC Solaar *(Photo by Philippe Bordas, courtesy of Sentinel Ouest, © 2000)*

Assassin (DR courtesy of Assassin Productions)

Massilia Sound System *(Photo by François Poulain, courtesy of Adam Production)*

Double Pee of the group SIYA PO'OSSI.X *(Courtesy of Michelle Auzanneau)*

Ndjassi Ndjass of the group SIYA PO'OSSI.X *(Courtesy of Michelle Auzanneau)*

"Pochoir" *(Courtesy of Alain Milon)*

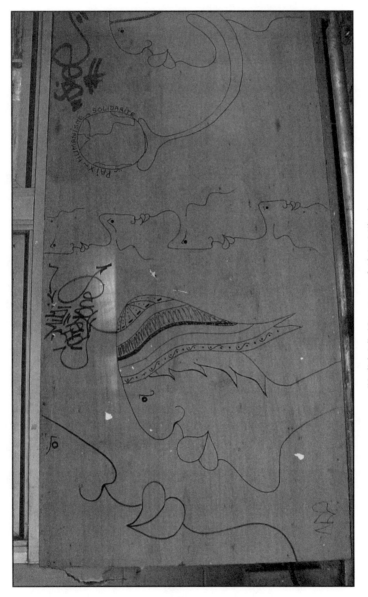

"Solidair" (Courtesy of Alain Milon)

any other, with a technique and a mastery of pictorial tools. But tags are also the sign of a *presence*, the presence of anonymous authors, inhabitants, visitors, travelers, wanderers, and foreigners in transit. Who, then, are these authors-actors who contribute to the modification of the City's landscape?

THE TAGGER AND HIS/HER REASONING

Tags fill spaces, but this filling is no appropriation. "Decorating" a wall or a fence is certainly occupying a space in a way that can be more or less legal, but this occupying is not the sign of an appropriation by that taggers in France do not mean to appropriate a territory (contrary to what is happening in other countries). In leaving their marks by occupying public space, taggers act with a sense of urgency. Their sole criteria are visibility and the duration of that visibility. While making a mess of a place, taggers are conscious of the fact that their work will be erased as quickly as possible. A hunter/hunted relationship is established, particularly obvious in the relationship that the taggers and graffers maintain with the employees of public companies like the RATP (Parisian public transportation) and the SNCF (French National Railways). Taggers know that their "work" will not last and that their short-lived mark, while fully participating in the different transformations of the City, also contributes to define some territorial occupying. To tag quickly, in the greatest possible number of places, to make sure that tags will be the most visible while being incomprehensible: such is the paradox of taggers, who wish to be seen while remaining impenetrable.

Here we are far from the idea of marking a territory; taggers are simply interested in making their marking last as long as possible. Unlike the North American urban tradition in which tags, even more than graphs, border a specific territory, "blocks" and tags in France do not aim to delimit a space, with few exceptions. They may be painted anywhere, even if some spaces are more tagged than others.[2] The same can be said for socioeconomics: there is no target population for the taggers, even if there is some correlation between tagged areas and certain socioeconomic criteria such as the quality of housing, the presence of special education areas (ZEPs),[3] the rate of unemployment, and the PCS and SECODIP levels.[4]

Taggers' reasoning may seem to be somewhat paradoxical. While seeking the most visibility, their mural expressions function as a sort of exchange of codes between the initiated. Tags are incomprehensible except to those who want to make the effort to decode them. There is thus a kind of visual dialogue between members of a community, the urban community. But behind these different postures, questions about the behavior of the tagger remain. The simplest, and the one that first comes to mind, is the esthetic logic: Do tags belong to the tradition of mural painting?

In the 1980s, the press reduced this question to phrases such as: "art or vandalism." Any response to this kind of question would be as pointless as the attempts at determining esthetic classifications. Tags exist; they are fully integrated into different urban expressions and as such they must be taken into account. The next step is to try to classify this mode of expression according to some scale of values. I will also set aside these philosophical and psychological questions about tags as expressions of a "graphomaniacal" and "glossolalical" behavior.[5] On the other hand, the social question is worth considering: do tags, like murals, impact the urban landscape, and as such do they contribute to the altering of the social bond?

Tags can be interpreted as a sort of signal sent to the City's institutional players, a simulated dialogue using two different languages between two players. On the one hand, the City representatives try, each with their own methods, to respond to the multiple malaises of urban life with the creation of meeting places, neighborhood centers, a network of associations and teachers, etc. On the other hand are the taggers, who express their feelings, their hatred for and their perceptions of the City. We therefore have two kinds of reasoning, two modes of understanding, two divergent languages, and, when all is said and done, two actors who occupy the urban space differently and without ever meeting. To return to the metaphor at the beginning, we can say that the City and tags will never be the skin or the medium of the other. If the City has many different looks and a changing soul, tags do not want to be reduced to urban fabrics, whatever esthetic value is granted to them.

Behind this search for the greatest possible visibility is hidden a more complex approach to the urban reality, an approach that questions the public space as organized by the City. Tags occupy the City's places, among them the street, without this presence being reduced to a simple territorial occupying. I have already described these mural expressions as "traces without spaces" primarily because they are ephemeral and, as such, they never belong to the history of a place, but also because these mural expressions seek above all to translate a fluidity, a movement, and a mobility. They are not intended to be affixed to a wall. These expressions remain without a "ground" for they are without a real author, without an origin, and without a defined place. Tags are intended to question the nature of the social bond staged by the City. To do this, I will first turn to the street as a geographical space and physical medium for tags in order to question subsequently the breaking down or building up of the public space.

DOES THE CITY HAVE A FACE OR A LANDSCAPE?[6]

The City has a face, but also a landscape. Here, face and landscape express two different things, even if each is absorbed by the other. Accordingly, should tags and murals be considered as expressions of the City's face, or as elements of its landscape? The face is often the most expressive part of the City's body, whereas the landscape seems to be but a simple extension of this body. Nevertheless, doesn't the urban landscape also seek to incorporate the City completely, to take it over to become a face? In fact, the City seems to have a face whose body would be the landscape. They are both pieces of the same entity. Perhaps this is how we can best describe the City: a face and a landscape that merge together to form a whole, a particular space. The question is to know how tags and murals are situated in this urban landscape. Are they, because of their visibility, the City's funny faces, or are they merely scars disfiguring a landscape?

One can argue that this landscape corresponds to the City area, i.e., with the walls, buildings, or monuments being merely accessories with plans defined by the addition of construction, intersections, or neighborhood organization. Isn't it rather a global vision, a sort of urban map that would take into account the architecture of buildings, the arrangement of frontages, signs, and historical heritage, i.e., everything that explains the City's various mutations?

Rather than reducing the City's landscape to a simple geographical area, it seems more interesting to consider the City's project. Yet, this consideration is not in the sense of a plan meaning a spatial representation nor as a more or less enlightened vision from engineers mechanically splitting up a territory, as was the case with the "new cities," in which, rather unintelligently, modernity meant house blocks and modular structures. On the contrary, the project plan expresses the manner in which the City organizes its combinations to integrate its various parts to make up a whole. Such is the feeling that one gets in certain neighborhoods of Paris where, from one street to another, the landscape is completely different but still perfectly integrated into the body of the City. This plan, unique in its topographic composition, constitutes the internal and external structure of the City, a kind of visible body: in other words, the City's skin.

As this plan is built up, how should tags and murals be considered? As visual expressions artificially added on to the City's specificity and, as such, as an external and short-lived mark, as scars to some extent disfiguring the City's body, or as pigments of the City's skin? Either skin or scar, it matters little in that each choice is based on a scale of values. Tags and murals truly pose a series of problems to City inhabitants. By accepting them or valorizing them, they become an institutional means of expression, even though they want to be acts of resistance. By condemning them we make them a mark whose illegality is proportional to its washability.[7] In both cases, we ignore the problems that they are supposed to express.

Whether the City's skin is more or less esthetically harmonious with a more or less painful body scar, tags invite us to wonder how the City shows itself to its inhabitants. The City dresses, covers, and recovers itself with layers as diverse as they are ephemeral. All of these different layers partly make up the body of the City. The City would thus have a face that would change from place to place, and the various kinds of tags would be as many translations of the City's smiles, funny faces, or grins. These translations are questions that demand our attention, such as the quality and harmony of buildings, their integration into the urban space, and the respect for their inhabitants. They are also expressions on the very edge of the City skin whose many scars are more or less successfully accepted by the body.

Let me now explain why tags are not indifferent to the City's players. First, let us say that both the City and the taggers do not want to be each other's physical medium. Just as the City will never simply be a medium for tags, tags cannot be reduced to the urban space. Tags are in the City but they do not want to be the City's unique expression; their medium is urban and their expression impregnates the City, even if the City would rather stage these visible forms that translate urban dysfunction.

These mural signs question everyone, from the simple inhabitant to the local elected officials. If they provoke many different reactions, it is in part because they hurt our desire for cleanliness and property.[8] These scars on the City's clean skin are felt as foreign and degrading marks (here we are far from the idea of a body enhanced with scars, and expressing power). Tags or murals on a building or a storefront are attacks on private property, a real but also symbolic aggression of a social player (the landlord or "bourgeois" for private places, administration officials for public places). However, the taggers' reasoning cannot be reduced to this simple fact. Perhaps they never even think about it, as they often only think about the maximum "visibility" of their work. Thus we abandon a political line of questioning—calling on politicians by expressing urban malaise and endless shortcomings—in favor of a narcissistic and advertising meaning: To show one's face, signature, and graphs to the largest possible public, all the while making them incomprehensible.

THE STREET: THE NATURAL PLACE FOR TAGS

The street is above all a place for circulation, transit, and networks, a place that allows the comings and goings, a sort of vital artery or lung without which the City could not breathe. I previously discussed the body and the skin of the City, but the street is also where people rush. "Rue," "ruelle," "ruer," "ruade:"[9] everything in these words evokes movement, but movement on a human scale and not the mechanical displacement of the buses or tramways that require more space. Even if people rush in the street, they do so at their own pace. It is in the City's streets—and this is where we can see a difference with the countryside—that the moments of "passerbiety" are created. These are moments during which the passersby, the inhabitants, evaluate and appreciate their own movement, moments when they translate their movement into a transit, moments that also allow them to build their own definition of place and territory. Henri Lefebvre considers the street a place of living; in fact, he speaks of it as a "spontaneous theater" (29), a place in which people are just passing by and a place that intelligently combines every type of spectacle possible. Everything is linked and the street is a theater whose passersby are in turn authors, actors, and spectators of their own play. In this space, everything is on the human scale. Even if the movement is violent and oppressive, it remains in the range of what people agree to do with it. This does not mean that the street does not have its own history, but rather that it acts as if it were a place outside a territory, a place with no definite stability; in other words, a moving place.

The street has a history that is written in the buildings that define it, and even if it is delimited by its numbers, it gives the impression that it is in continuous evolution. The street and the landscape that comes out of it are not only moments of localization but rather spaces of potentiality, and the atmosphere that comes out of it contributes to building up the spirit of the street, a particular feeling that the passersby feel when they survey it. Although familiar, this feeling is also never the same and varies with each new visit. If the street exists in a geographical space, its combinations offer a place that each person can appropriate for him- or herself. Theater of life, theater of the street; the networks of the City present combinations that its conceivers had not imagined.

Even if the street is designed according to a plan, its wealth is beyond the plan. It exists only for those who wander in its streets, a little like Marcel Proust who, in his masterpiece *In Search of Lost Time*, punctuates his analysis of the places that he walks through with specific potentialities: Venice, Paris, or Combray. The street thus offers its specificities to those who survey it, and with each visit it presents different forms of movement. In this context, it seems logical that taggers choose it as an essential place of expression. A place of passing-by, the street, more than the avenue or the boulevard, offers a visibility that is a function of the passerby's moving pace. It allows him or her to discover, read, or decipher the various marks presented. As such, the street enables the City to breathe while it makes it possible for tags or murals to exist. To a certain extent, it becomes a sort of public place that makes a singular form of expression public.

The street offers taggers a particular space of expression, making its unique territory a place of transit that nevertheless remains immobile. In their "Traité de Nomadologie" (Treaty of Nomadology), Gilles Deleuze and Félix Guattari define the nomad as a person who, by reason of his very strong attachment to the earth, moves without going away; in other words, a human being who does not travel (315–423). How, then, can tags translate this particular attachment to a place and how can this attachment structure the City? Tags are indeed inscribed within a territory, but this inscription is of a particular kind. It also determines spaces without places in the sense that they really occupy a space (façade, wall, shop window, etc.) but this occupying, by its ephemeral nature and its movement, belongs to no one. Tags are made up of multiple layers put on top of and next to each other. These layers, added to the singular nature of the calligraphy used, make the whole incomprehensible, and thus we do not know what they mean (do they have a meaning?), who made them (do they really have an author?), and if they were made to last (is there any logic behind their creation?). And yet they exist!

TAGS AND MURALS: RECOMPOSING THE PUBLIC SPACE

Tags can be said to be works of art that are either meaningless or wholly artistic. However, such alternatives can lead us to a never-ending debate on the esthetic value of works of art and their measurability. It is much more interesting to question their meaning. In his chapter "Kool Killer, or the Insurrection of Signs" from *Symbolic Exchange and Death,* Jean Baudrillard examines the meaning of this type of mural expression. Recognizing in them neither denotation nor connotation, these visual forms—empty signifiers for Baudrillard—have no meaning, and they even dissolve the very signs of the City (76–84). Without trying to valorize this form of expression and without taking into account any esthetic context, let us say that these shapes, by their existence, raise the question of the occupying and the delimitation of public space. Whether they are accepted or not, they contribute to the definition of the public space, and as such are as important as any other visual indicator. Resting on value judgements leads us nowhere; on the contrary, seeing in these forms the expressions of dissolution or recomposition of the social bond seems more interesting. The advantage of these marks is that they make the social players question the consequences of such a presence. Beyond the different generalizations of the problems of the *banlieues* (inner cities) and the malaise of life in cities—with tags measuring this malaise—it seems more useful to reflect on the sociolinguistic context of this mural expression.

Tags possess an *expressive* content in the sense that, no matter what the circumstances are, they express something and they manifest a well-being or an illness. From this point of view, they are not devoid of meaning and even if they contribute to the dissolution of the City's signs, they succeed in saying something by this dissolution. According to the typology established by John Searle in *Expression and Meaning* (1979), in these conditions other qualities can be added to these visual forms. One could also say that tags are *assertive*; in other words, they signal how things are to the rest of the community, even if taggers feel all the pain in the world in saying it. At the very least, taggers translate their perception of the City and their condemnation of the urban shortcomings, like the absence of dialogue in the organization of urban development.

But this expression is also *promissive* in the sense that it defines the scope of a political program. Claiming no political slogan, taggers attempt to establish a program with contours that are rather vague. Its coherence matters little; the only goal is the presence of such a realization. More than free acts, tags fit together like a sort of political program with a personal reading, by their authors, of the social reality; they have a theme and they translate, in their own way, this social reality. Perhaps the most important aspect comes from the *directive* nature of these mural expressions, in the sense that they require the players of urban life to react and to intervene. From this point of view it is possible to displace the perception of this phenomenon to make it evolve while considering tags to be simple sprayed signatures that are detrimental to murals.

Without reducing the problem to one of an esthetic valorization, murals thus have a greater likelihood of being recognized and considered, by the majority of the City's inhabitants, as an integral part of the urban landscape if we consider tags to be simple visual pollution. Without defining as such the normalized spaces attributed to graffers so that they can express themselves—like the RATP did in the 1990s when it offered four-by-three white spaces—the recognition of graff as a mural art all its own can contribute to its acceptance by the urban community at large. Such is the case in certain North American cities like Los Angeles, where mural art responds to a pictorial tradition that is largely accepted. This is also what can be seen, albeit for other reasons, in large metropolitan areas like Paris where storekeepers, exasperated by the tags that cover their metallic shutters, ask the graffers to decorate their storefront according to specific themes. Done for reasons that are more esthetic (the shutters cease to be dirtied by the tags) and economic (the owner no longer needs to repaint his storefront regularly) than cultural (the mural fresco is not entirely a street art in the European tradition), the graff thus becomes a means by which the passerby becomes used to these new visual forms.

It is the beginning of a sort of esthetic education that has the benefit of familiarizing the City's inhabitants with these extremely particular graphic thematics. In these conditions, to say that tags pollute murals has the advantage of forcing people's frame of mind to evolve and to give a little more credit to the graffer since it valorizes his work.

But once again the esthetic perspective, which we earlier refused in order to evaluate these mural expressions, has the benefit, if it is managed well, of proposing a didactic approach that might lead the City's inhabitants to measure more effectively the nature of the social malaise that these marks express.

NOTES

1. The stencil starts with cutting out a piece of paper from a motif that is stuck to a support and "sprayed" with the aid of aerosol paint. Miss-Tic's stencils, for example, appeared on walls of Paris in 1985. They presented a woman's body with texts that varied according to the circumstances: "Les désirs hantent les désirantes errantes" (Desires haunt the wandering [female] desirers), "Fendue défendue" (Forbidden crack), "Les faims de mois sont difficiles" (My hungers are difficult; a play on words with "les fins de mois," the end of one's monthly budget), "Je joue oui" (I play, yes; a play on the words "je jouis," I come), "A ma zone" (In my zone; a play on the word "Amazone"), "Exilée volontaire d'un continent sans nom j'écris dans la marge de mots dits" (Voluntary exile of an unnamable continent, I write in the margins of spoken words; "mots dits" is a play on "maudit," damned), "Des murmures impatients prennent la parole sur la voie publique" (Impatient murmurs find their voice on the public stage; a play between the words "voie" and "voix," voice), "Transgresser les frontières, désorganiser l'ennui, s'inventer des passions, travestir les clichés. Miss-Tic Présidente" (Transgress frontiers, disorganize boredom, invent one's own passions, disguise clichés. Miss-Tic for President; the name Miss-Tic is an obvious play on the word "mystique"), or "J'ai des frissons tatoués sur la peau" (I have shivers tattooed on my skin). See Miss-Tic, *Je ne fais que passer*, and those of Blek, with his rats, and Jérome Mesnager and his white and stylized human forms.

2. In a survey conducted in 1999–2000 on tags in Paris for the Parisian Graffiti Observatory, Paris's *arrondissements* (districts) were divided into five areas based on the frequency of tagging. From the most tagged to the least tagged, they are: 1. 11th, 10th, 18th; 2. 20th, 9th, 3rd; 3. 19th, 17th, 15th, 14th, 13th, 4th; 4. 2nd, 12th, 6th; 5. 1st, 8th, 16th, 7th, 5th. A more detailed map allows one to be more precise as to the exact nature of the places marked with tags, as the

---

taggers' logic has absolutely nothing to do with the administrative divisions of the *arrondissements*. Tags are placed where they will be the most visible and around public places like, for example, high schools.

3. *Zone d'éducation prioritaire* (translator's note).

4. PCS = *Profession et catégorie sociale* (Profession and Social Category); SECODIP is an institute in charge of socioeconomic studies.

5. See Alain Milon, *L'étranger dans la Ville. Du rap au graff mural.*

6. Note the proximity of the French words for face ("visage") and landscape ("paysage") (translator's note).

7. The washability of an inscription is currently the sole judicial criterion that allows us to define the contraventional or correctional nature of the infraction. If the inscription is washable, the tagger risks a minor fine (article R 38 of the Civil Code). If the inscription is only somewhat washable and results in a defacement of the medium, the penalty is correctional; this is defined in articles 257 (for public property) and 434 (for private property) of the Penal Code. These articles have been replaced by articles 322.1 for crimes committed on private property (fine of up to 25,000 francs [approximately \$3,600] and penalty of up to two years in prison if the defacement is non-indelible), 322.2 for public property (fine of up to 300,000 francs [approximately \$42,850] and penalty of up to three years in prison), and 322.3 for acts committed collectively (fine of up to 500,000 francs [approximately \$71,400] and penalty of up to five years in prison).

8. Note the similarity between the French words for cleanliness ("propreté") and property ("propriété") (translator's note).

9. An untranslatable play on words between "street" ("la rue") and "to rush" ("se ruer") (translator's note).

WORKS CITED

Baudrillard, Jean. *Symbolic Exchange and Death.* 1976. Trans. Iain Hamilton Grant. London: Sage Publications, 1993.

Deleuze, Gilles, and Félix Guattari. *A Thousand Plateaus: Capitalism and Schizophrenia.* 1980. Trans. Brian Massumi. Minneapolis: U of Minnesota P, 1987.

Lefebvre, Henri. *La Révolution urbaine.* Paris: Gallimard, 1979.

Milon, Alain. *L'étranger dans la Ville: Du rap au graff mural.* Paris: PUF, 1999.

Miss-Tic. *Je ne fais que passer.* Paris: Editions Florent-Massot, 1988.

Proust, Marcel. *Remembrance of Things Past.* Trans. C. K. Scott-Moncrieff and Terrance Kilmartin. New York: Knopf, 1982.

Searle, John R. *Expression and Meaning: Studies in the Theory of Speech Acts.* New York: Cambridge UP, 1979.

8

Hip-Hop Dance: Emergence of a Popular Art Form in France

Hugues Bazin
Translated from the French by Lars Erickson

Among the hip-hop disciplines, dance is undoubtedly the expression that best allows the understanding of the development of hip-hop in France. It sheds light on the place of a popular art form and on the stakes that connect it to contemporary society. Though artistic disciplines may be, to an increasing degree, byproducts of the culture industry, hip-hop dance reminds us that one cannot reduce the meaning of a practice solely to its economic aspect.

THE BEGINNINGS OF A COLLECTIVE HISTORY

Indeed, if rap today has great economic clout, it may be worth remembering that at the beginning of the 1980s dance was the training ground for most of the rappers in France. At that time, moreover, it was not yet conceivable to rap in French. Let us also note that private FM radio stations (known in France as *radios libres*), first created in 1981, constituted another hip-hop training ground where DJs experimented with "sounds coming from other places," as one commonly says.

The media treated hip-hop as an adolescent craze. They only saw manifestations of a trend in the explosion of dance practices between 1984 and 1985 thanks to the broadcast of the show *Hip-Hop*, hosted by Sidney (first on a public radio station, then on a television channel). As a sort of dance floor, cardboard flourished in the entryways of buildings. An entire generation, captivated by the esthetic of body language, sought to reproduce it in a spontaneous and enthusiastic way. Evenings in cabarets, competitions, and other battles represented ideal settings for collective emulation. Once the Sidney show had ended, the appearance seemed to confirm the media's vision of hip-hop as a passing fad. There is, however, a difference between the end of visibility and the movement of a popular emergence.

It was the low point in the movement and many stopped dancing. Some turned to rap or professions in the cultural arena; others found work in completely different sectors. Still others, less fortunate, who had given up everything for dance and who had earned money putting on performances, were not able to accept the fact of being relegated to the shadows after having been in the spotlight, and they fell into delinquency. Finally, some stuck with it, giving lessons or organizing events while continuing to dance, training in the backrooms of neighborhood centers and putting on small shows on local stages. Even though isolated in their region, these "old guys" were going to become the pillars of a dance renewal and were going to pass their wisdom, acquired at great cost, on to the following generation. While many national institutions produced the first large-scale shows in the early 1990s, more and more dance courses were given in sociocultural structures. Thus, if a first juvenile wave had receded down staircases and nightclubs, another, more mature one had returned ten years later to submerge contemporary theaters and sanctioned cultural centers. Few people at the time were able to notice this ebb and flow and to measure the amplitude that the movement was going to take. Today, France is one of the rare countries accommodating so many professional and nearly professional hip-hop dance companies.

AUTONOMY OF A CULTURE

The young explosion of the 1980s and the constitution of professional companies in the 1990s relate back to different moments of visibility: mainly intimist or media-focused in the first case, more institutional and economic in the second case. Very often, the commentators and critics cling only to those periods that are illuminated by artificial lights. If the latter moments indicate recognition of the hip-hop form, that does not mean that they are better understood and accepted. It is a paradox peculiar to France. On one hand, the number of hip-hop dance festivals and the financial assistance for their creation give evidence of the support of cultural centers and public officials. On the other hand, the strong institutional presence immobilizes the practices and expressions within a semantic, symbolic, and historic frame that evades the initial participants.

Aside from a few ecological niches, there are very few autonomous spaces so that a living culture can structure and re-appropriate the meaning of its relationship to the world and develop an independent commentary on the world. The developmental processes appropriate for a form, the precise relationship between the physical and the intelligible, between the group and the individual, between tradition and modernity, between transmission and creation, between awareness and diffusion, between repetition and innovation, between conformism and experimentalism, in short, everything that constitutes the interest and the power of hip-hop as a popular art form, all that remains hidden in shadows.

POPULAR ART

One is not born hip-hop, one becomes hip-hop. That acquired freedom in the work, in a certain relationship to the production, constitutes a characteristic of the popular form. After years of practical experience beginning in the 1980s, a professional consciousness refined the techniques. The precision of the movement and the rigor of the engagement are all the more sought out by those who want to make hip-hop dance their craft. A vocabulary, a common set of material, and then a repertory have now been transmitted from one generation to another.

Different styles of hip-hop dance borrow from different vocabularies both traditional and modern. Break dancing is a part of hip-hop dance made up of figures on the ground with preparation for the drop (top-rock). The dancers establish a new hierarchy in the role of body parts by modifying the main support points. Thus, rotations on the head (head spin, tracks), on the hands (ninety-nine, scorpion, thomas) or on the back or shoulders (cup, crown) liberate the legs from their role as carriers. The six-step is the basic footstep for the tricks that allow, based on the imagination and virtuosity of the dancer, art the transition between the main phases of the break. The upright part of hip-hop dance possesses a very wide variety of styles based on muscular contraction and relaxation (boogie, moonwalk, vogueing, popping, locking, pointing, micro-pulsion, tetris). It also borrows from gymnastics, combat dance (up-rock, capoeira, martial arts), jazz dance, and other modern influences that one also finds in the collective choreographies of hype.

But hip-hop dance cannot simply be enumerated as a series of movements or learned techniques (this explains the difficulty, after years of discussion, in the creation of an advanced degree accredited by the French Ministry of Education in hip-hop dance, even though such a degree exists for contemporary dance or jazz dance). All the creative play is found at the level of the articulations: between the details and the large phases, between upright dance and ground dancing, between references to academic foundations and research into varied domains, between work on the matter of form and the exploration of universes of cultural recognition.

The force and survival of hip-hop stems from that ability to develop interstitial spaces of cultural creation outside of institutional forms and to construct experiential routes where master-artists can be trained. Thus, hip-hop developed in France as a mesh-like network where each point constituted a history of meeting. This constantly worked and reworked form, where the artist defines himself more as an artisan, sheds light on popular culture. Indeed, hip-hop dance as an esthetic form finds its raison d'être not just in the pleasure of watching it. It is not pure emotion detached from reality; on the contrary, it brings us to reflect on our relation to the world. It informs us of a culture, a way of being, of individual and collective progressions, of the development of a thought and an intention.

Hip-hop culture transcends the singularity of each meeting by using a common language. By opening onto the physical world that places art at the center of life, hip-hop culture invites us to join the interstitial spaces where each is the author of his or her own practice. Hip-hop as a form is both codified in its structure and free in its access, archaic in its relation to the earth and its rhythm, modern in its individuality affirmed and constructed out of nothing, hence everything, using the basic matter of life. This way of bringing together a collection of elements into a unit producing meaning is another way of defining popular art. Demanding requirements push for the surpassing of the form itself and unveil the personality of the dancers to us.

MOVEMENT AND NARRATION

The richness of hip-hop dance in France stems both from the affirmation of original individual careers and also from the specificity of regional stylistic developments. The Paris regions (Aktuel Force, Black Blanc Beur, Boogi Saï, Choréam) and the Lyon regions (Traction-Avant, Azanie, Accrorap, Kafig, Art Mouv'in Silence) are considered cradles of hip-hop dance and their opposed styles allowed for the spurring on of emulative creativity. Yet, outside the large metropolitan areas, one now sees that all the French regions contributed in their own way: the Lille agglomeration (Melting Spot, Funk Attitude, Dans la Rue la Danse), Toulouse (Olympic Starz), Bordeaux (Révolution), Montpellier (Mega Cool Rap), Strasbourg (Magic Electro), Nantes (Hb2), and so on.

This stylistic diversity and this vitality of movement translate into an ability to combine space, energy, and technique. The alliance of freedom and work, of fluidity and form, of subjectivity and structure releases an esthetic power. The different dance styles express this tension between being and matter. The form becomes hip-hop in its awareness of this craft where movement can constitute a matrix of messages, of representations of the world, of rules of life, of values, of abilities.

The narration can follow an initiatory route and draw the unusual geography of Earth-Mother whose temple is the stage. Manifestation of a mystery or the unveiling of a truth, a revealing energy in the religious sense lays out the cardinal points of a force field. Art, both primitive and spiritual in its ability to work on primary elements that then acquire a symbolic dimension, hip-hop reintroduces here a culture of enchanted relationships to the world.

Other narrations play on the border zones. These borrow from the symbolic of network; follow the course from one bank to another, of the voyager, of the nomad, of the foreigner. They dislodge us from our path by indicating another way to cross the world. The scene opens onto a distance that comes toward us, an otherness that resembles us, particularities that push toward the universal. Among the influences that are North American, Caribbean, African, and those of migrations and immigrations, of social particularisms, of regional colors, the art of collage, of borrowing, of re-appropriation, engages us in a rhizome-culture of floating roots taking from here and there its creative substance.

The social satire of the dominated can represent another path of the narration. It reminds us that hip-hop is akin to an art of combat, of deflection, and of reversal. From capoeira, to West Indian dances, martial arts, and street breaking we find again and again the fundamental role of popular art as a culture of resistance confronted with the processes of control and alienation.

PUBLIC SPACE AND NEW THEATER

Another way to resist domination is to play on many spaces in alternative ways. One can attend choreographic centers and continue street practices. That ability to invest many levels of accessibility, many types of stages, is also the essence of a popular form. It is a way to evade the evolutionary characteristics that the dominant culture attributes to the popular culture; that is to say that hip-hop emanates from the "bottom" towards the "top," from the social towards the artistic, from the street to the theater. This way of qualifying dance companies as "issued" from hip-hop would mean that hip-hop is but an intermediary category in the ascension towards "true dance." This esthetic assignation to a point of origin (social and territorial) leads to an explanation of artistic work before its public reception. This is typical of a desire to control the symbolic, esthetic, and economic aspects of the production of cultural emergings.

Hip-hop dance companies do not consider the "street world" and the "art world," to borrow the expressions Howard Becker uses in *Art Worlds*, in terms of an opposition. Choosing one over the other would be giving up on either the experimentation of artistic research or the collective development of popular education and culture. Now, the principle of popular art is the power to play with these two tendencies in order to heighten the demands (rigor of work, quality of reception, desire to learn) not only for an elite but also for an entire population (artists, amateur performers, audiences, supporters). Thus, for the dance companies, professionalization does not mean the passage from one universe to another, but rather the ability to increase the mobility and the dynamism between the two because of a double legitimacy. The one, of a cultural order, is a recognition in relation to their equals as referent ("master") in the hip-hop movement. The other, of an artistic order, is a validation in relation to institutions as dancers-choreographers with the financial support of the dance company.

The individual does not cease to be "hip-hop" by changing spaces beginning with the moment when the form keeps its same principles of social and cultural structuration. This is the example of circle and freestyle: a collective redistribution of sociocultural space-time where the audience becomes actor in an open stage by being invited to enter into the dance circle. It is a place for the expression of free figures, of competition, of validation of skills, of appreciation of mastery where the stylistic influences of the moment are measured, but also where the entry codes are learned within the circle of an esthetic family. It is here that a transmission takes place, a live apprenticeship through a means of exchange that is similar to the economy of the gift (accessibility, unity, individuality). The challenge through free-style and improvisation is the privileged moment of a collective experimentation. What is also called performance, takes up again the concept of a work in movement where the processes turn out to be as important as the end result.

The first scene begins in urban space without going through academic codes, the examination of spaces dedicated to culture by culture. From the street scene to that of contemporary theater, dancers integrated other restrictions while seeking to preserve their freedom. Access to theaters does not sanction an ascent of street dance to the stage, but rather a descent of the stage to the public. Today, hip-hop art within the theaters favors movement of audiences, a decompartmentalization of genres, and a re-appropriation of the esthetic relationship between work, artist, and audience. The artistic dimension opens a space in life by restoring to the collectivity the ability to develop esthetic communication usually reserved for experts, critics, and the media. The popular arts are rarely considered fine arts because, according to Richard Shusterman, by qualifying as esthetic the judgment of taste and the experience of beautiful and sublime, theoreticians also try to develop and to reform these experiences in certain directions.

The place of hip-hop dance brings us back to the question of "living spectacle," its contemporary range and significance as a public forum and location of constitution of new esthetic frames of references. It is up to the public to judge that function of art which is to enlighten us on the complexity of a reality in movement, to bring us access to an intelligent vision of being engaged in the world. The attainment of a certain way of being takes precedence over the accomplishment of a final work. It is a vital balance, tense, precarious, ephemeral.

WORKS CITED

Becker, Howard Saul. *Art Worlds*. Berkeley: U of California P, 1982.
Hip-Hop. TF1 [Télévision Française 1]. Narr. Sidney. Produced by Laurence Touitou. 1984–1985.
Shusterman, Richard. *Pragmatist Aesthetics: Living Beauty, Rethinking Art*. Cambridge: B. Blackwell, 1992.

9

Rap in Libreville, Gabon: An Urban Sociolinguistic Space

Michelle Auzanneau
Translated from the French by Ralph Schoolcraft

Rap first appears in Libreville, Gabon, at the end of the 1980s and grows significantly in the 1990s. Most of the groups are from the country's lower and middle classes (the majority in Libreville), though one of the pioneering groups represents an exception: the members of V2A4 come from the country's most privileged class. Whatever their origins, however, like in the United States and Europe, Libreville rap music is tied to contestation by young people who decide to fight social injustice and in so doing participate in the evolution of their society. As on these other continents, this social movement is also accompanied by the effects of rap's trendiness. Each working class neighborhood has several rap groups and many young people have joined the movement as actors and listeners.

Libreville rap thus draws on the American tradition and is influenced by the European movement as well (the French groups, in particular). Libreville rappers feel that they share experiences and aspects relative to their living conditions with their French peers and especially with their American counterparts—for instance, they see certain ties with respect to the African community's painful past of colonization and slavery. In addition, like most of Gabon's young people, they valorize certain European cultural and behavioral models. Enjoying even greater success are the American models that, as in the European case, reach Libreville by way of (and thus are filtered through) the media and schools.[1] "Getting out," "getting ahead"; these phrases sum up the aspirations of a young generation that idealizes the Western way of life and suffers from the contradictions of their "developing" country.

Born in the 1970s, Libreville's youth grew up in the midst of the social, demographic, economic, and physical upheavals brought on by the city's rapid urbanization in the years following Gabon's independence (Pourtier). A magnet from within and without the country, the city saw its population increase due to the various migrations. But, as with other cities (Agier), Libreville faced the development of informal urbanization and the precarious dwellings of the people's neighborhoods. Organized previously on the basis of ethnic neighborhoods like most other new African cities, Libreville then became a place where populations and cultures were jumbled together and the lineage system was gradually abandoned in favor of other types of social organization.

Yesterday's social and cultural distinctions break down and mix together in the city as the distinguishing criteria for today are born. In effect, the city moves in the direction of the uniformization of values and behaviors as well as toward their differentiation. With the opening up of social networks and the complexification of social relations, "symbolic families" appear, serving as the basis for new solidarities and social distinctions (Agier, 35).

At century's end, traditional and modern social behavioral models, cultures, and identities exist side-by-side in Libreville. The young generations, who never experienced the pre-urban or village sociability of their elders, are resolutely turned toward modernity. They reject the values and traits of this prior sociability, which they perceive as archaic and ill-adapted to the realities and needs of a developing society. In this still-evolving social space, the population's identities are deconstructed and (re)constructed. Libreville's youth believe that they possess their own culture, *une culture métissée* (a mixed culture). This culture has built itself by integrating elements coming from traditional and Western cultures that young people "recontextualize" in their urban setting, as a way of appropriating these elements. It expresses the plurality of the new generation's cultural identity. The youth see this new identity as being that of modern urban Africans (and Gabonese in particular), and feel connected to one or many of its cultural elements. Depending on the context of a given communication or exchange, the youth adopt behaviors distancing them from or bringing them closer to traditional and modern models. They negotiate in this manner the valorization of a particular facet of their identity.

This behavior stems in part from their use of different languages and their linguistic varieties. Though their number differs according to the categorizations used, in Libreville, ten or so linguistic families subdivided into several languages are spoken, in addition to others present due to migration (such as those coming from Central and West Africa).[2] None of the country's languages enjoys official recognition, with French alone being designated as the national language. The standard European French represents the sole linguistic norm. Gabon's population possesses no local language for facilitating interethnic communication, which thus takes place in French. French is used in a great number of circumstances, in both public and private domains. Subject not only to exogenous but endogenous norms as well, local usage presents departures of varying degree from standard exonormic French. Though the endogenous norms do not possess any official legitimacy, the departures from standard French nonetheless serve as factors of social differentiation and thus of identification. They therefore are attributed "identiary" values that can come into play during certain exchanges.

The vernacular languages are used for intraethnic and informal communication. Their transmission from one generation to the next is not always assured, particularly when the parents are not of the same ethnicity. The loss of vernacular languages thus plays to the advantage of French.

Cities—and Libreville is a particularly flagrant example—are characterized by multiculturalism, multilingualism, and multiple ethnicities. They become the space of expression and creation of new identities, new cultures. As a product of cities, rap repeats their characteristics to a certain extent and, by staging them in songs, offers us elements for interpreting and thus for understanding urban phenomena. For this reason, rap has attracted researchers in the human sciences. One has only to look at the number of articles and books published on rap in the 1990s to gauge scholars' current interest.

In sociolinguistics, the problematic of rap is tied to that of the city. Scholars interested in the causal relations existing between urban factors and linguistic practices consider rap as an urban discourse that could provide much information on this subject. Studying the songs and, to a lesser extent, the overall daily linguistic practices of rap artists, these scholars see rap as a space of communication marked by the specificities of the musical genre. However, current research has not pursued this avenue far enough, for these specificities have only been partially examined since the interdisciplinary nature of the studies is more an "interdisciplinarity of juxtaposition." This overlooks the fact that the social, musical, and linguistic dimensions—among others—of the songs are interrelated and call for a "pluridisciplinary approach of collaboration."

There are many more European and American studies on these questions than in Africa, where rap as well as the city is a more recent phenomenon. In France, scholarship on rap music is tied to questions concerning the French suburbs, *cités* (housing projects), and migration. Their studies on rap show that the music is a result of the marginalization of young people, coming for the most part from migrant families.[3] Often caught between two cultures and languages, youths in the newer generations find themselves in search of an identity. Rap is seen as "the result of a young generation's quest for identity taking place in an interstitial cultural situation in which they produce the attributes of their own culture" (Calvet 1994: 274). It is characterized as "a movement of identiary and cultural recomposition" (Billiez 1997: 71), and as the space of elaboration of a linguistic code characterized most notably by the composite aspect of its lexicon and functioning as an emblem of the pluralistic identity of the youth.[4]

What is the status of these problematics in the African context? What are the characteristics and functions of rap music in Libreville, whose urbanization and the resulting social processes do not seem to have reached a level of stabilization yet, and whose new cultures and identities do not seem to have reached maturity? What sociolinguistic dynamics does rap music reveal and drive?

These questions are part of an ongoing sociolinguistic project examining rap music in Dakar and Saint-Louis (Senegal), Libreville, and the Parisian suburbs. The principal hypothesis guiding my research is that rap, as a social movement and urban discourse, reveals certain urban sociolinguistic dynamics at the same time as it takes part in them. Rap can be seen as the space of expression, circulation, and creation of the urban youth's behavioral models, some of which are of course linguistic. In this sense, rap plays a role similar to that of the city, acting at once on the form of, the symbolic and social values of, and the functions and varieties of languages and their varieties.

My investigation is ethnographic in nature. It consists of an immersion into the daily life of young rappers in order to better capture their realities, and to talk with them about different aspects of their personal history, their activities as rappers, their prospects for the future, as well as their perception of their sociolinguistic context. In addition to my audio recordings and notes accompanying the observations and interviews, I have collected numerous songs in both written and musical form. To date, I have assembled 163 songs coming from nineteen groups, with eighty-one of the songs belonging to ten Libreville groups. (Among these latter, there is also a clan, that is, a group of bands.) I have also collected the songwriters' own representations of their linguistic productions within the songs. This research was done in 1998–1999 for Senegal and in 1999 for Libreville.[5] As a work-in-progress, these results are provisional, but they nonetheless indicate some directions for interesting work. The analyses presented in this essay pertain only to Libreville rap and in particular to the interactions proper to their songs. My research is interested not only in the songs but in the interactions that take place around them as well.

The analyses of the songs have been carried out on three levels: the enunciatory (pronouns, terms of address, etc.), linguistic (the forms and reasons for choices of languages), and sociocultural (content, external context). In light of the pages available to me here, I will limit my presentation to a few important points on the characteristics and meanings of the linguistic practices in these songs.

The population sample I interviewed in Libreville was primarily composed of men between the ages of seventeen and twenty-eight in 1999. (There were only two women, both solo artists.) Most were in secondary or higher education and belonged to the ethnic groups Fang, Téké, Punu, or Nzébi. Generally, they were born and raised in Libreville, and joined the rap movement between the ages twelve and twenty-one. At the very most, the reputations of these groups or solo artists are national; usually, they are only locally known. Some have put out or participated on one or even several records.

Rap in Libreville can be seen as one of the "symbolic families" for urban youth. This family extends beyond the country's borders, to an international scale. Nevertheless, the very foundation of rap music is to speak out in the name of one's community, i.e., in the name of one's country, city, neighborhood, or "posse." Representing them leads the songwriters to anchor their message in the daily realities of their society. For these reasons, rap engages two types of solidarity: a solidarity uniting them with the international hip-hop community; and a solidarity that unites them with the society in which they live.[6] Expressed in part linguistically, these solidarities reinforce the influences of the be-havioral models already present in the city. The forms and uses of the languages and their varieties in the songs (as well as in the names of the groups and the rapper's monikers) express these solidarities and in-fluences. They also demonstrate the plurality and variability of the identities negotiated by these rappers, who are first and foremost social subjects.

Thus, of the ten groups and solo artists interviewed, five use En-glish—alone or with another language—in their names. The names of these groups are: Bad Klan, New School, Professeur T., Slûûm dûûm ("the glory of the slums," borrowing the English term), Siya Po'ossi X (where "possi" draws both on the English "posse" as well as on the Fang phrase "siya possi," which means "land to be knocked down," i.e., lands or peoples to be killed, a polemical reference to the fate of Africa over the centuries).

As for the monikers, generally designed and functioning as displays of the rappers' identities, they allow for even greater possibilities of ex-pressing one's solidarities and the mix of identities being asserted by the rap artists. Often multilingual, they mix English, vernacular languages, and French. Each part of the pseudonym refers to a characteristic of the rapper: a personality trait, a group to which he or she belongs (family, clan, etc.), behavioral habits in or out of the rap scene, etc.

> Example: *Double Pee* (P-P) *Endeigne Mebe Me Ndong Eke*
> P: *Parfait*, "perfect" in French, the first name of the rapper in question
> P: *Pivot*, which refers to his dance style, but also to "pediatrician," which in Libreville designates men attracted to adolescent girls.
> Endeigne: "grandson of" in Fang
> Mebe Me Ndong Eke: "name of his grandfather."

The choice of a particular part of a pseudonym acts as part of the rap-per's identiary strategy in the framework of a precise context.

> Example: *Pee* will present himself or be presented as "Double Pee" or "Pee" when his identity as a rapper is the focus of the song. The other components of his name will appear to indicate his ethnic or, more fre-quently, national identity.

The songs allow the expression of such strategies because they constitute themselves as the place of "enunciatory stagings" in which characters, or "sociotypes," interact in specific contexts (of space, time, etc.).[7] The addressees of the songs' enunciations can be figured both within the text (a participating sociotype) and outside of it (the audience). The success of the songwriters' strategies within the song is relatively certain insofar as they are the only producers of the speech "exchanged." These strategies go beyond the frame of the song's specific dialogues, however, since for the rap artist the object is to negotiate one's identity with a large audience and in so doing position oneself socially.

The recurrent sociotypes in Libreville rap are: the rapper, in all the different facets of his or her identity (member of the posse, family, ethnicity, neighborhood, clan, etc.), and the members of the posse (his "brothers," for instance); rappers from other posses; the powers-that-be (the political class, administration, the privileged class); "whites" (the former French colonizers); and the Gabonese social subject. With the exception of the posse members and especially the rapper, the sociotypes receive negative or ambivalent characteristics. Other rappers are dismissed as fake and whites in power portrayed as exploitative or corrupt, etc., while the Gabonese are portrayed as their brothers-in-suffering but also as being oblivious to the causes of their difficulties, and fighting the rappers rather than the authorities. In the instances where negatives traits are attributed to the rap artist or posse members, these traits in fact have a valorizing effect on their image (Auzanneau, 711–34). The relations defined by these sociotypes are relations of alliance or conflict. Moreover, the rapper always appears in the songs (through the subject pronouns "I," "we," or "one"; the monikers; or terms of kinship) and is the principle enunciator, while the other sociotypes appear as more or less direct addressees (for the most part by way of second person pronouns, injunctive forms of verbs, or through insults).[8]

Among the eighty-one Libreville rap songs collected, forty-one are monolingual in French and six are solely in a vernacular language (Fang, for the most part). The others alternate between languages, notably French and English (ten), French and one or more vernacular languages (seventeen, with Fang again being the most common of the latter), French and a migration language (one song uses Lebanese Arabic), or a mixture of vernacular languages (six, generally Fang and Téké). Their song repertoires present two typical cases as to the choice of languages: some groups strongly favor French to the detriment of vernacular languages whereas others give vernacular languages an important place while still using French. The first instance is the most frequent, yet certain signs—statements, changes in repertoires, the choices of pseudonyms and music—seem nevertheless to indicate a tendency toward affirming Gabonese identity and culture and thus toward an emancipation from Western models. When the exclusive or preferential selection of French is not a question of competence in vernacular languages or owed to familial linguistic habits, it usually is motivated by a desire for an international "career." Making oneself known outside of one's country means using one of the languages of mass communication. This explains in part the choice of English. However, English is never used on its own in any of the songs; it always coexists with French.

In the instance of those rappers who do draw on vernacular languages, this usage is still less frequent than that of French or the codic alternation of French and English. With most groups, this is only done in a few songs (though some groups set themselves off through their more extensive use of vernacular languages as an affirmation of Gabonese culture). The choice of a vernacular language is most often associated with that of another language, usually French—and never English. The most frequent alternations consist of inserting one or several relatively short vernacular segments (or a refrain) in a song written for the most part in French.

> Example: Lliazz, a female Fang solo artist, in "Je m'assume" ("I'll answer for myself").
> [In French]: *Now that I've found out, ooohh, I'll answer for myself* (Voice of an old storyteller of *Mwett* [traditional Fang tales]): *Bamba mon ne ka yi èèèèèèè yeu mon aa yi* ("Pretty baby, don't cry, tell me, does a baby cry?").[9]

The choice of vernacular languages in the song is motivated by the identiary function of these languages. As a vehicle for the values of traditional Gabonese society, these languages symbolize Gabonese identity more than any ethnicity. They allow the songwriter to express solidarity with the Gabonese community, adhesion to cultural values that could revalorize the rapper's image in the eyes of adults, and to mark her or his difference with respect to a France that is perceived as economically exploitative, culturally assimilating, and a former colonizer. Within the rap movement, which puts Gabonese culture on a public and perhaps even international stage, vernacular languages are enjoying something of a revalorization. Formerly associated with out-of-date and archaic values (and thus with "backwardness"), these languages are now becoming languages of "authenticity" and "roots" and thus claim for themselves an identiary role both in rap and in the city. The vernacular languages are used in treating themes concerning Africa, rap, or dimensions of the author's personal experience.

Standard French and English (also exonormative) are also used for treating the most serious or formal subjects, as well as topics concerning the way of life of young city dwellers. These languages best bear the ambivalent values of Western society: they are simultaneously the languages of development and of deculturalization. A sign of culture and formal education, French well learned thus indicates high social status, too. For young Libreville rappers, standard French is the language of the other in the sense of John Gumperz's "'they' code" (as opposed to a "'we' code"), on which Louis-Jean Calvet draws (1994), followed by, among others, Billiez (1997), and Cyril Trimaille, in order to talk about representations of this same variety in the case of French rappers. However, if ethnic languages, in opposition to French and English, are seen as "'we' codes," they are not the ones that best match the urban youths' identity. Their mixed identity, which they situate in the interstices between cultures and languages much like French suburban youths in another context, corresponds to another French. This French is recognized by young people as a "'we' code" that serves as a vehicle for the expression of the values to which they adhere and as a symbol of the traits of the group to which they belong: that of young Libreville city dwellers.

Example: an excerpt from the song "To Kill La Wana" by Siya Po'ossi X.[10]
"Here's the rotten neighborhood,
"Late at night, at midnight, we love the night,
"We don't like the Police or trouble,
"*L.B.V. by night*, it's the life of pussies there to be scratched
"At the seaside where flesh is sold top dollar,
"*Business*, you'll eat from the sweat of your ass,
"The earth belongs to those who work it,
"At the seaside, these riff-raff, they're working it
"Who would disagree? Who gets the fee? How much ya gonna give me?
"The *bizz* on patrol, a patrol of big limp dicks
"The hookers scramble, La Wana finds it funny,
"A *blue brazza* runs into me,

"He stinks of *bosh*, he's drank too much,
"In his eyes I read, 'My wife cheated on me,'
"*Djogué me za bîme wa!* (Fang for "Clear out or I'll punch you")
"I managed to lose the *mwan Bizz ma*,
"I'm running, I don't have any more *pia*, I'm far from home,
"I jump in a *tacla*: we ride, ride, ride,
"In my neighborhood now, the *Depa*, I don't pay,
"I light out in the *mapana*,
"That's how it is, *abana*,
". . . even the police go to *Yogo santé*,
". . . they've *zouacké* without even paying."[11]

The lexicon in this excerpt includes:

- phrases borrowed from English: "L.B.V." (an acronym for Libreville pronounced "elbivi"); "by night," "business";
- non-standard phrases from French (slang, popular speech): "chatte" (pussy, slang for female genitalia, a metaphor); "tacla" (taxi, composed from an apocope of taxi and resuffixing); "racailles" (riff-raff—in this case, prostitutes); "putes" (prostitute, apocope of "putain"); and terms of insult such as "grosses couilles molles" (literally, "big soft balls," but in the emasculating sense of slang phrases in English for "flaccid penis");
- popular French terms in Libreville derived from: a) local languages: "bizz," "biz ma" (police in Fang); "mwan bizz ma" (child of the police in Fang); "abana" (leave a taxi without paying), from "mandingue a banna" (it's over); b) unknown origins: "pia" (money); "mapana" (people's neighborhood, shantytown); c) semantic processes of transformation acting on units of diverse origins: "brazza bleu" (police, which combines the French term for blue with a brand of cigarettes, Brazza, whose package is the same color as the police uniform); "bosh" (local beer, an antonomasia of the name of a local brand of beer); "yogo santé" (designates by contiguity a place of prostitution situated next to a dairy factory bearing this name);
- a neologism belonging to the Wenteck lexicon of the Siya Po'ossi X, consisting of a combination of neologisms in the production of "zouacké" (screwed, from "zouacker," to screw or fuck, derived from the Creole term of the same meaning [zouk] but with the introduction of supplementary vowels).

This variety of French is of the same family of urban varieties developed by young city people in Africa or on other continents, such as the Noutchi of Abidjan (Ivory Coast) or the French of some of France's suburbs (Calvet 1999: 41–42). These linguistic varieties are characterized by the use of a monolingual syntax and a composite lexicon. The base language is subjected to the influence both of the exogenous norm and of endogenous norms—it undergoes a relexification that can be endogenous (as in the case of slang) or exogenous (Calvet 1999: 45). These varieties fulfill identiary and, in some cases, encrypting functions. Libreville's relexified French is the product of exogenous and endogenous influences that manifest themselves in the form of borrowings from Gabonese languages, languages of migration, and English (standard and non-standard, but especially slang). It also results from the use of a non-standard French lexicon rich in argot forms (*verlan*, metaplasms by addition or subtraction, etc.) and of Libreville popular speech and neologisms.[12] Generally speaking, this lexicon is used by young urbanites (those adhering to the rap movement in particular), but some forms function like markers indicating that one belongs to a specific group (that of rappers, for instance). Youths thus distinguish between "rappers' language" and "young people's language" on the basis of certain neologisms, or English and French slang forms (*verlan* in particular). These linguistic units are marked by their forms or by the semantic fields to which they refer (notably, the urban youth's way of life, music and rap in particular).

In addition, the songs using this variety of French often contain interphrastic, intraphrastic, or extraphrastic codic alternations, and thus the resulting phrases are a form of code-mixing.

> Example: In the same song, "To Kill La Wana": "I'm speeding through the *mapana,*/ that's how it is, *abana,*/ gniène kiri engalene bezzima be ngadzeng ma (at sunrise the police were looking for me)./ the following morning they were looking for *La Wana* . . . / I've become a fugitive/ *ma ké ma mare mbii* (I take off running)."

As with the lexicon, these *métissées* (mixed) phrases are not used in all situations or with the same frequency.

Usage varies from one songwriter to another, with the particular usage that a given songwriter makes of certain categories a sign of his or her specificity: one will use more French *verlan*, fewer phrases borrowed from local languages (e.g., Encha'a of Slûûm dûûm), while another relies more extensively on local languages, forms specific to Libreville French, mixed derivations and English (cf. Siya Po'ossi X). These specificities are part of the songwriters' styles as well as their ideologies and social positioning. It is a question of situating themselves as being first and foremost Gabonese, or a modern urbanite, etc.

But usage also varies within a rap artist's or group's repertory. Changing from one song to another or from one part of a song to another, these variations are owed in part to the esthetic and musical constraints of a song, but they also depend on the situational givens and social norms of linguistic behavior in place in a society. Thus, for example, a songwriter uses French phrases more or less close to standard French according to a song's themes, the relation established with the listener, and the goal sought by the songwriter.

The production of phrases containing mixed and relexified forms of French correlates most often with rap themes (socioeconomic misery, sociopolitical critiques, followed by sexual relations, social and health scourges, or personal reflections). It rarely corresponds to themes of mysticism, and never to that of tradition, these latter being subjects generally reserved for vernacular expression. These mixed forms are also frequently used when the relation to the listener is conflictual, and especially when the songwriter articulates this conflict by subjecting his or her addressee to symbolic verbal attacks and humiliations. Bragging on the part of the rappers tends to draw on these composite forms as well. In these instances, the phrases mainly use non-standard French and English, often in the form of insults.

But for these songwriters it is not just a matter of producing more or less standard French phrases or of playing with the role given to mixed phrases. It is also a question of varying the number of lexical items coming from each category. For example, the place given to English terms or French *verlan* can diminish in favor of terms taken from Libreville French or local languages when the songwriter wishes to negotiate his or her Gabonese identity through the interactions being represented in the song. As with the languages in which they originate, these lexical units are vehicles for particular symbolic values that the speaker mobilizes in a given phrase.

As with the mixture of languages that often accompanies it, relexified French is being explicitly revalorized in rap circles. Outside of the rap scene, these linguistic forms signify deculturalization, adherence to values not accepted by traditional society, a devalorized social status, etc. Since they can only be implicitly positivized by the young generation, they undergo a revalorization in rap that follows along the lines of the process of "stigma reversal" described by Billiez (1997) in her analysis of the French spoken in France's suburbs. This reversal has not yet taken place outside of their networks. This is probably due to the fact that rap as a social space produces its own behavioral norms and "legitimacies" (in Pierre Bourdieu's sense of the term), which are occasionally in opposition to those at work in society. Globally speaking, this relexified French has several functions, which we can term identiary and emblematic; stylistic; and pragmatic.

In the case of the identiary and emblematic function, the relexified French expresses the two types of solidarity at work in rap songs, one at times subordinating the other in certain phrases, depending on which lexical items are privileged. In using this linguistic variety, speakers mark their attachment to Gabonese culture at the same time as they mark their break with the values of both their own traditional society and the dominant Western society. This variety is the emblem of the rappers' culture and of their *métissée* (mixed) identity as young urbanites. On a stylistic level, the relexified French can be associated with informal discourses, an unbridled style considered particularly appropriate to the behavior of young rappers and the expression of conflict. Finally, in terms of pragmatism, the relexified French leads to specific verbal actions vis-à-vis one's public.

Even though it poses a few comprehension problems for a portion of the Gabonese population, the lexicon employed by the young rappers does not really fulfill an encrypting function, for this would not correspond to rap's aims. Paradoxically, the relexified French serves the purpose of provoking communication with a pluralized public. It is a question of striking listeners' attention, as a means of putting oneself on the public stage as a speaker (Auzanneau, 711–34). The encrypting thus only serves an identiary function through ostentation. Moreover, these lexical choices correlate perfectly with other linguistic choices tied to the enunciations (e.g., subject pronouns, terms of address, fixed formulas), languages and their varieties present in the song. They also match up with the song's semantic plot as well. These elements work together and reenforce one another in such a way as to participate in the global and progressive meaning of the text.

Example: The song "To Kill La Wana" cited above (114–15): This song is structured semantically in five parts with a refrain.

As for the linguistic choices:

The first part sets the scene ("Here is the neighborhood." "How much ya gonna give me?") and furnishes the descriptive elements of the nocturnal world. The discourse is impersonal. The songwriter, La Wana, does not appear as speaker in his discourse, with the only personal pronouns used being the impersonal or general *we* ("we love the night"); *you* also in impersonal forms ("You'll eat from the sweat of your ass") or in reported speech ("How much you gonna give me?"); the impersonal *it* ("Who does it work out best for?"); *they* (referring to the prostitutes); and the interrogative pronoun *who* ("Who would disagree?"). As we noted previously, the lexicon presents phrases lifted from English and several French slang terms. The songwriter draws on some fixed formulas ("The earth belongs to those who work it"), one of which is modified ("You'll eat from the sweat of your ass"). The local setting is established only by the denomination "L.B.V." and the mention of "the seaside."

In the second part ("Les *bizz* en patrouille . . . je suis loin de chez moi"), the songwriter recounts the police raid on the prostitutes and the altercation between the police and La Wana. The discourse is now personalized. The rapper takes on a central role in the discourse through the multiplication of the pronoun *I* and the use of the pseudonym *La Wana*. The discourse becomes anchored in the local setting and more direct: the lexicon specific to Libreville French appears whereas English terms disappear; a segment in Fang is introduced by way of an interphrastic alternation; and several statements use direct reported discourse in which terms of insult help represent the conflictual relation.

The third section, beginning with I jump in a "*tacla*," deals with the police search for La Wana and thus is also centered on the rapper and locally anchored. It presents the same characteristics as the second part. The last two parts of the song broach the subject of police corruption and the policeman comes gradually to occupy a place equivalent to that of the rapper: the pronouns and denominations referring to each are just as frequent, the local French lexicon decreases but the introduction of segments in Fang increases and even ends the song.

Just as with the choice of languages, the lexical choices depend upon an ensemble of situational parameters and correlate with the other choices on linguistic and other levels (musical, poetic, etc.).

As occurs outside of the song, in daily life, and as studies on code-switching have shown,[13] speakers make these choices in light of the languages' values and functions. The linguistic units chosen and the implication of their choice within a given context and the goal they are pursuing in this communication also figure in prominently. For the rappers, it is a matter of negotiating through language a relation with the addressee and a specific identity at the moment at which they intervene and choose to speak. In the changing urban society of Libreville, where different social groups and cultural models coexist, rappers are inserted into large networks of communication that confer upon them a plurality of identities (as members of a country, continent, neighborhood, posse, etc.). The diversity of languages with their variants, along with their mode of functioning as markers of identity (of being Gabonese, African, or an urbanite), allows the speaker to privilege in a given exchange one of the facets of her or his pluralistic identity toward a given communicational goal.

In the songs, the choices are generally conscious, depending in part on poetic and musical constraints. In keeping with Billiez's approach (1998), I consider these choices to be "intentional" since they take place during the compositional phase, and thus constitute a deferred speech act with respect to the act of reception. They therefore cannot be linked to "identity acts" characterized, on the contrary, according to R. B. Le Page and Andrée Tabouret-Keller's definition, by their spontaneity. Perhaps one could speak in certain cases of "intentional identity acts"?

Though only partial, these first results provide a few elements for reflection. They demonstrate that the study of rap is a means of examining the relationships between urban processes and sociolinguistic situations. It reveals current sociolinguistic dynamics and some of the motors generating them, particularly in that it allows one to identify values and functions of the languages and their varieties not just within songs but inscribed in a given sociocultural context.

In addition, as a specific social space occupied by young people, rap becomes the locus of circulation and, eventually, of transformation of the values and behavioral models, some of which are linguistic, originating within and without the country. It is a space for the expression of cultures and identities under construction. Lastly, it is itself a space creating these identities and cultures, as well as codes and linguistic units that will ultimately be put into circulation beyond the songs. Rap thus reveals and participates in the unifying gregarity of the city's activities, and works with the city on the form, functions, and values of its languages.

A deeper appreciation of the phenomena at stake in rap music would be most useful. One direction for further study would be to compare linguistic practices in and around the songs. And, finally, it seems indispensable that other, correlated studies in the human sciences produce data enabling a common, progressive analysis as we work together toward a better understanding of multidimensional objects such as rap, or, on a larger scale, cities.

NOTES

1. See Jannis K. Androutsopoulos and Arno Scholz who treat the phenomenon of cultural globalization in the context of their study of European rap.

2. The linguistic families are Pygmy and especially Bantu, with the varieties commonly identified being Punu, Nzébi, Fang, Mbédé, Kélé, Miéné, Kota, Kandé, Séké and Vili (K. Boucher).

3. See, in particular, Louis-Jean Calvet (1994), Jacqueline Billiez (1997, 1998), and Cyril Trimaille.

4. See Calvet (1998), Billiez (1997), Trimaille (1999), and Médéric Gasquet-Cyrus et al.

5. Investigating French rap will be my next step. This will be part of a collective inquiry, research on France and certain aspects of Senegalese and Gabonese rap having been redefined in the collective and pluridisciplinary framework of the research group GRAFEC (Groupe de Recherche Appliquée aux Formes d'Expression Contemporaines), founded in January 2000 by Margaret Bento (Université de Paris V) and myself. The results presented here are the fruit of my own analyses.

6. I have adapted to the Libreville context Calvet's notion that French rap affirms solidarity with respect to the community of American rappers and relative to the geographical origins of the migrant populations (Calvet 1994: 277).

7. Florence Casolari adapts the notion of enunciatory and sociotype stagings from (respectively) Robert Vion (1994) and Jacques Brès.

8. The rap artist is the principal enunciator *globally* speaking, though this is not necessarily the case for all sections of the song.

9. The Fang spellings are that of the lyricist Lliazz.

10. *Translator's note*: The text of the song is in French with English and vernacular terms (mostly Fang) interspersed. Words appearing in English and in vernacular terms in the original are marked in italics.

11. "Voici le quartier pourri / tard le soir, minuit, on adore la nuit / On n'aime pas la Police et les ennuis / L.B.V. by night, c'est une vie de chattes qui se grattent / Au bord de la mer où la chair se vend chère / business, tu mangeras à la sueur de tes fesses / la terre appartient à ceux qui la travaillent / Au bord de la mer ces racailles, elles travaillent / qui en disconvient? A qui cela revient? Tu

paies combien? / Les bizz en patrouille, une patrouille de grosses couilles molles / Les putes s'affolent, La Wana trouve ça drôle / Un brazza bleu me tombe dessus / La bosh il pue, il a trop bu / Dans son regard, j'ai lu 'ma femme m'a déçu' / Djogué me za bîme wa! ("laisse-moi sinon je te frappe," Fang) / j'ai semé le mwan Bizz ma / je cours, je n'ai plus de pia. Je suis loin de chez moi / J'emprunte un tacla: on roule roule / Arrivés dans mon quartier: la Depa, je ne paie pas / je trace dans le mapana / c'est comme ça abana / [. . .] même les policiers vont à Yogo santé / [. . .] ils ont zouacké sans même payer."

12. *Translator's note*: Verlan is a French slang form used primarily in the Parisian suburbs that consists of reversing the order of syllables or even consonants within a word. Example: *tomber* (to fall) becomes *bétom. Verlan* itself is a transposition of *l'envers* (backwards).

13. On code-switching, see John Gumperz or the work of Joshua Fishman, and the research that follows up on their themes, such as that of Carol Myers-Scotton.

WORKS CITED

Agier, Michel. *L'invention de la ville: banlieues, townships, invasions et favelas*. Amsterdam: Archives contemporaines, 1999.

Androutsopoulos, Jannis K., and Arno Scholz. "On the Recontextualization of Hip-Hop in European Speech Communities: A Constrastive Analysis of Rap Lyrics." *Americanization and Popular Culture in Europe*. Ascona (Switzerland) International Conference (10–14 Nov. 1999). http://www.archetype.de/hiphop/ascona.html. 18 July 2001.

Auzanneau, Michelle. "Identités africaines: le rap comme lieu d'expression." Special issue of *Les Cahiers d'études africaines* 163–164, XLI, 3–4 (2001): 711–34.

Baker Jr., Houston A. *Black Studies, Rap and the Academy*. Chicago: U of Chicago P, 1993.

Billiez, Jacqueline. "L'alternance des langues en chantant." In Jacqueline Billiez and Diana-Lee Simon, eds., *Alternance des langues: enjeux socioculturels et identitaires*. Special issue of *Lidil: Revue de linguistique et de didactique des langues* 18 (1998): 125–40.

———. "Bilingualisme, variation, immigration: regards sociolinguistiques." 2 vols. Qualifying dossier to become Research Director. Université de Grenoble III, 1997.

Boucher, Karine. "Langues et identité culturelle des jeunes librevillois de 15 à 30 ans: une enquête de terrain." D.E.A. Thesis, Université de Paris III, 1998.

Boucher, Manuel. *Rap, expression des lascars: significations et enjeux du rap dans la société française*. Paris: L'Harmattan, 1998.

Bourdieu, Pierre. *Questions de sociologie*. Paris: Editions de Minuit, 1984.

Brès, Jacques. "Le Jeu des ethnosociotypes." In *Lieux communs: topoi, stéréotypes, clichés*. Ed. Christian Plantin. Paris: Kimé, 1993. 152–61.

Calvet, Louis-Jean. *Pour une écologie des langues du monde*. Paris: Plon, 1999.

———. *Les voix de la ville: introduction à la sociolinguistique urbaine*. Paris: Payot & Rivages, 1994.

Casolari, Florence. "Constructions stéréotypiques dans le rap marseillais." In *Parole et musique à Marseille*. Eds. Médéric Gasquet-Cyrus, Guillaume Kosmicky and Cécile van den Avenne. Paris: L'Harmattan, 1999. 73–92.

Gumperz, John Joseph. *Discourse Strategies*. New York: Cambridge UP, 1982.

Jacono, Jean-Marie. "Pour une analyse des chansons rap." *Musurgia* 5.2 (1998): 65–75.

Le Page, R. B., and Andrée Tabouret-Keller. *Acts of Identity: Creole-based Approaches to Language and Ethnicity*. New York: Cambridge UP, 1985.

Moussirou-Mouyama, Auguste. "Norme officielle du français et normes endogènes au Gabon." In *Une ou des normes? Insécurité linguistique et normes endogènes en Afrique francophone*. Eds. Louis-Jean Calvet and Marie-Louise Moreau. Paris: CIRELFA, 1998. 421–36.

Myers-Scotton, Carol. "The Negotiation of Identities in Conversation: A Theory of Markedness and Code Choice." *International Journal of Sociology of Language* 44 (1983): 115–36.

Poplack, Shana. "Conséquences linguistiques du contact des langues: un modèle d'analyse variationniste." *Langage et société* 43 (1988): 23–48.

Pourtier, Roland. *Etat et développement*. Vol. 2 of *Le Gabon*. Paris: L'Harmattan, 1989.

Trimaille, Cyril. "Le rap français ou la différence mise en langues." In *Les parlers urbains*. Ed. Jacqueline Billiez. Grenoble: Université de Grenoble III, 1999. 79–98.

Vion, Robert. "De l'hétérogénéité des instances énonciatives." *Cahiers du français contemporain*. Paris: Didier, 1994. 227–45.

DISCOGRAPHY

Siya Po'Ossi. X. *Mapane Groove Act. 1*. Quartier 10 / Siyafrikafonk, 1996.

Siya Po'Ossi. X. *Mapane Groove Act. 2*. Quartier 10 / Siyafrikafonk, 1997.

10

The Cultural Paradox of Rap Made in Quebec

Roger Chamberland

At the end of October 2000, six rap albums were among the twenty best-selling records in the United States. Of these, seven million copies were sold by Eminem alone in the first week of release, an all-time record for any kind of music. Yet this Eminem album encourages homophobia, promotes violence against women, and disrespects law and order. This album, as is the case for the five others figuring at the top of the charts, carried the warning label that states, "Parental advisory. Explicit lyrics. This album may offend some people." At the same moment, *Newsweek* featured Dr. Dre and Eminem on its cover and also presented a substantial article on rap (Samuels et al., 58–66). In that issue, we learned that 41% of *Newsweek* readers occasionally listened to rap music. Of that number, more than 75% considered rap as being violent, encouraging a negative attitude toward women, insisting too much on sex, and finally promoting, to great excess, materialist values. Quite a somber portrait of a musical genre born a mere twenty years ago in the impoverished suburbs of New York that then grew rapidly in popularity everywhere in the world. As Adam Krims notes, American rap has been taken over by local collectivities and has given birth to new musical structures negotiating, as much on the musical side as on the written side, its belonging to a hegemonic form as well as to specific local issues. Krims writes, "I will put forth an argument that the sonic organisation of rap music—both the rapping itself and the musical tracks that accompany it—is directly and profoundly implicated in rap's cultural workings (resistant or otherwise), especially in the formation of identities" (2). However, this local specificity can be the focal point

124

of many different factors such as age, race, gender, social class, or any other significant category with which a collectivity contrasts itself to American rap, whose hegemonic tendency accords authenticity only to rap emanating from within its geographical space. Krims was quite right in his appreciation of American rap as a reference point from which homologous forms have spread to nearly all corners of the globe. However, if we want to evaluate more closely the resistance of a hip-hop community, one that chooses to stay at a distance from some white-culture indigenous forms rather than integrating them, we should then consider the question from a broader angle. To put it another way, rap appears to be a musical form inherent to crossbreeding.

In this essay, I would like to analyze the situation within Quebec society where rap presents itself as a cultural paradox and where the rap scene is dominated by groups with members coming from ethnic communities while rap music is listened to largely by white French Quebecers. This is even more of a paradox since it is very difficult, even impossible, for white French groups to attain some legitimacy if they do not display a certain ethnic hybridization. Quebec occupies this particular position at the crossroads of French, American, and Canadian rap and thus I can better define the paradoxical situation of rap in Quebec. To seize that musical dynamic I will present a brief outlook at the historic evolution of Canadian rap and then Quebec rap in order to sense better the cultural paradox that characterizes rap musical culture in Quebec.

THE EMERGENCE OF RAP CULTURE

Rap music was slow to develop in Canada, due partly to the fact that ghettos are rare even in the largest Canadian cities, where Canadian rap was born. Unlike in the United States, Canadian rap soon moved away from black communities, and had a reverse "integration" effect, with its fashions, slang, and behavior being adopted by predominantly white, middle class youth. From the very beginning, word of mouth and live concerts were the best way to spread this black urban art form, or "Black Noise" to quote Tricia Rose's expression. Despite its growing popularity in the United States, rap was introduced only gradually in Canada, gaining new listeners thanks to the initiative of a few people living within black communities, mostly from Caribbean backgrounds, in Toronto, Halifax, and Montreal, where the first rappers emerged. These initiators—MCs Supreme, Brother A., Sunshine, and Ebony Crew—performed successfully on the local scene, but never recorded. In the mid-1980s, the major Canadian record labels showed no interest in black music in general. At the time, a general misunderstanding and rejection of this type of music and its audience was keeping rap from taking off.

But new management and production enterprises devoted to promoting rap music were eventually created. For example, Beat Factory Productions and Management in Toronto, founded by Ivan Berry, enabled Michee Mee (Michelle McCulloch) and LA Luv (Phillip Gayle) to record a number of singles, "On This Mike," "Elements of Style," and "Victory Is Calling," on the British label Justice Records. Michee Mee, who is a native of Jamaica, was considered for a while to be the major hope of Canadian rap. Her performances as the opening act for LL Cool J, Salt-N-Pepa, and Sinead O'Connor in Toronto and Montreal brought her recognition and enabled her to sign recording contracts in New York and London. For Berry, it was Mee's ragga-style rap that made her typically Canadian because Canadian rap at the end of the eighties was a harmonious mix of rap and reggae due to the important Jamaican population in the Toronto region at that time. Despite the advantages Michee Mee enjoyed in the production and distribution of her albums, her career was limited to Canada and she did not succeed in the U.S. market.

In 1990, the first Canadian rapper to achieve any degree of international success was Maestro Fresh-Wes (born Wesley Williams in Toronto of Guyanese parents). He was backed by a large Canadian recording company, Attic, who had decided to test the rap market. Wes's album *Symphony in Effect* sold more than 150,000 copies and his singles "Let Your Backbone Slide" and "Drop the Needle" were given extensive airplay on alternative radio. They were even heard on a few commercial stations, due to their similarity to MC Hammer and Vanilla Ice, who were having their period of glory in the same year. Soon other rappers, such as MCJ, Cool G, HDV, and the better known Dream Warriors, began to break onto the scene and succeeded beyond the Canadian borders. MCJ and Cool G were a duo from Montreal consisting of James McQuaid and Richard Gray, both natives of Halifax, whose rhythm and blues–influenced style ensured that two of their singles, "So Listen" and "Smooth as Silk," enjoyed reasonably wide distribution. In contrast, the provocative, pornographic rapper HDV (Sean Merrick, from Toronto), in tracks like "Pimp and the Microphone," rapped about the harsh conditions in which black people were living in Canadian cities. But the Dream Warriors were most successful on the international scene, thanks to Ivan Berry from Beat Factory Productions, who signed them to Island Records' London-based label. Even though they were little known in Canada, the Dream Warriors (Louis Robinson and Frank Albert, alias King Lou and Capital Q, both from Toronto) had three high-rating singles released from their album *And Now the Legacy Begins*, "Wash Your Face in My Sink," "My Definition of a Boombastic Jazz Style," and "Ludi." These songs assured them of exposure first in England, then in the rest of Europe, and finally in the United States.

The Dream Warriors' music and lyrics were highly eclectic and seductive, partly due to the presence of a constant melodic line. A number of other groups, including Simply Majestic, Krush and Skad, Main Source, RazorBlayd, Top Secret, Slinky Dee, Self-Defence, and K4ce (K-Force), all of whom consisted of black musicians, soon evolved, attempting to follow in the footsteps of the Dream Warriors' success. But white rap crews were also quick to respond to the spread of hip-hop in the mid-1980s. The Shuffle Demons from Toronto released the rap-inflected singles "Spadina Bus" and "Out of My House Roach" in 1986 and 1987, which were among the first Canadian recordings on which scratching and recitative were used. The video clips of these tracks were given high rotation on Much Music, a Canadian television channel similar to MTV, partly due to their spectacular elements. The Shuffle Demons' music was primarily jazz fusion, which overlapped into other musical territories to obtain unusual sonorities. Right from their beginnings in 1984 they sampled television theme tunes, movie soundtracks, recent pop hits, rap tracks and jazz classics within the textures of their own original compositions. Laymen Twaist, a bilingual and multiracial trio from Montreal, made a brief foray into rap's sphere of influence with their rap version of Lou Reed's "Walk on the Wild Side," even if their album tended to privilege pop-rock. Kish (Andrew Kishino), from Toronto but of Japanese origin, also made his mark on the Canadian rap scene with his first recording, released in 1991, "I Rhyme the World in 80 Days." Produced by First Offence, a new production house created in Toronto, it gave evidence of the growth of a Canadian rap repertoire that involved a growing awareness of ethnic communities struggling against problems of oppression and racial tensions in the big Canadian cities.

If Toronto rapidly became the capital of Canadian Anglophone rap, Montreal is a hub of both U.S.-influenced Anglophone rap and Francophone rap deriving from French origins. But it would be misleading to say that the synthesis of these two styles, U.S. and French rap, which contain notable differences, took place through a simple transference of music and texts. The acclimatization of rap was strongly affected by the social, political, and cultural context of Quebec. In this province, more than 85% of the population speaks French, and political campaigns and acts of protest are carried out in ways similar to those of oppressed communities in ghettos in the United States. In 1987, the group French B from Montreal (Jean-Robert Bisaillon and Richard Gauthier) initiated the rap genre in Quebec with their hit single hit "Je m'en souviens" (I Remember), which addressed the issue of Law No. 101, addressing bilingualism. Three years later, the Francophone rap movement formed by Kool Rock, alias Ghislain Proulx, and Jay Tree, alias Jean Tsarzi, released "M.R.F. est arrivé" (The French Rap Movement Has Arrived), in an attempt to initiate hip-hop culture in Quebec. Stephan Chetrit and his song "Rapper Chic" (1991) did not contribute a great deal to the evolution of this culture since he proposed a watered-down version of rap similar to that of Vanilla Ice and M.C. Hammer. It was left to Maleek Shahid (John Morrow), a white Muslim based in Montreal, to reposition rap in its rebellious protest vein by writing politically committed tracks delivered in Spanish, French, and English. But lack of any commercial success failed to launch these rappers' careers, and they were largely consigned to anonymity.

On the whole, neither Quebec recording companies nor the major labels, with their relatively discreet presence in Quebec, have been prepared to risk producing rap albums. Commercial prospects are hazardous, given that many people judge rap only in the light of the scandals, murders, and arrests reported in the mass media. In Quebec, as well as in the rest of Canada, the production, distribution, and broadcasting of rap remains confined to the margins. Its evolution has been very slow and the major recording companies have yet to be convinced of its viability. In the year 2000, however, we should note that the situation has changed as evidenced by the creation of the VIBE-TV chain, a satellite station of Much Music, in Toronto, which plays exclusively clips of rap, rhythm and blues, and reggae, twenty-four hours per day and seven days per week.

RAP IN QUEBEC

Situated at the crossroads of U.S. and French music, Quebec rap had a recent boost with the release of Dubmatique's *La Force de Comprendre* (The Power to Understand), which combines soul music with a French hip-hop approach. French rappers like IAM, M.C. Solaar, Ménélik, Oxmo Puccino, Faf Larage, 2Bal2Nèg (with whom Dubmatique recorded a song) and NTM are well known in Quebec, and frequently broadcast on radio and television, demonstrating the viability of French rap in this Francophone city. Nonetheless, certain Montreal rap groups like Shades of Culture, Obscure Disorder, and Eye Spy Crew continue to perform in English, although their influence is restricted to the Montreal region. In contrast, Dubmatique's debut album sold 100,000 copies and succeeded in capturing the media's interest with two of their songs reaching the air waves: "Soul Pleureur" (Weeping Soul) and "La Force de Comprendre" (The Power to Understand). The reasons for their seemingly spontaneous success are many: the group's stage performances reveal a sense of spectacle that excites their audiences; they express an optimistic and humanist, even pro-religious view of life in their lyrics; and their music incorporates the sounds of soul and gospel. In "Soul Pleureur," the loss of a loved one becomes the pretext for a reflection on the injustices of life and a sense of culpability.

Using both English and French, Dubmatique appropriates the rhythms of French rap texts (such as IAM and M.C. Solaar's styles), where the refrains are often entrusted to soul voices, giving an emotional depth to the songs. Dubmatique is also a group that succeeds in synergizing its audiences; not in any aggressive way, but in a direct relationship, tinted with a certain seductive naïveté. The group, who won a Félix trophy for best alternative band at the ADISQ Gala Awards—Montreal's Francophone music awards—draws on the Senegalese and Parisian origins of two of its members, O.TMC and Disoul (the third member is DJ Choice, formerly of Zero Tolerance and Shades of Culture) as well as the influence of both U.S. and French rappers to produce a distinctively local, but also hybrid and international, form of rap, summed up in the title of one of their singles

"Montreal/Paris/Dakar." They also celebrate Montreal as a welcoming, multicultural city, open to all. Their songs "Un été à Montréal" (A Summer in Montreal) and "Jamais cesser d'y croire" (Never Cease to Believe) reinforce this image by concretizing Montreal's role as a focal point in a musical hybridization generated by hip-hop. With their ragga and soul-inflected rap and their politically and morally conscious lyrics, they are the first rap group in Quebec to succeed in breaking into both the Francophone and Anglophone national broadcast and recording markets, as well as getting radio and video airplay in France and the rest of Europe. They even performed as support to the teen-pop group the Backstreet Boys, reaching 180,000 people all over Canada, and their album was described in the Montreal French language weekly newspaper *Ici* as "making Montreal less of a small town and more of a city on the musical planet" (Anonymous, 13).

Markedly different than Dubmatique, the group La Gamic nonetheless features two of Dubmatique's members, DJ Choice and Barney Valsaint. The originality of La Gamic is due to the presence of two women, Pittsbury So and Natty Soyha (backed by Rakoon) who write and perform the group's lyrics. Each tells stories of her own life, fears, and anxieties, and defines rap and hip-hop culture as the new voice of a youth in search of itself, as in the track "Mine de rien" (Nonchalant). Unlike Dubmatique's soul music, La Gamic prefers scratching atmospheres sustained by a discreet melodic line following a drum beat. But like Dubmatique, La Gamic gives all they have got on stage in their highly energetic performances. Natty Soyha has also begun performing with Jean Leloup and Bran Van 3000, both of whom borrow elements of rap in much of their work. Of all the Quebec rock groups, Bran Van 3000 borrows from hip-hop the most. Their music is hard to define, as their eclecticism covers a broad spectrum from trip hop to funk, rock, and punk, but in the background, we hear clearly the work of a DJ playing turntables, which often serves as a diving board for the rhythm. Another group attempting to follow in the footsteps of Dubmatique is Les Messagers du Son (LMDS, The Messengers of Sound). Their influences are far more French than American. What all these groups have in common is that they emerged from the suburbs rather than the city centers, and above all from the surroundings of the island of Montreal where neo-Quebecers install themselves, creating ethnic ghettos that are not necessarily characterized by poverty, but by racial conflicts.

The situation in Quebec City is very different. The relative homogeneity of the population (more than 95% of the population is white and/or French) shifts the focus of rap to the demands and protests of youth. The group Eleventh Reflektah capitalizes on a complex and very refined recording process, all computer generated, of samples ranging from well-known film themes (such as Ennio Morricone's "Once Upon a Time in the West") to tiny fragments, not more than one or two bars, of classical and contemporary music, through to snatches of traditional Quebec songs. Unlike many other groups, Eleventh Reflektah does not employ scratching, except sometimes in live shows, when DJ Nerve, one of the best DJs in Canada, performs on the turntables. The group's first EP was successful in Vancouver and Seattle and earned them recognition by Beat Factory in Toronto, who will include an Eleventh Reflekta track on their next compilation. The group has opened for Rascalz, Thurst, and Dr. Frankenstein in Quebec City, and they have been praised for their elaborate compositions. A group, later named La Constellation, composed of Deux Faces-le Gémeaux and producer Kassis—both white and French and raised in the suburbs of Quebec—has signed with Tacca Records, one of the pre-eminent record companies in Quebec, and has produced *Dualité*, an album that has enjoyed some success without really imposing itself. These white rap groups have little chance for success because they lack the ethnic authenticity that resides in a certain cultural difference.

This is particularly the case in Montreal, which has become over the years a musical space where ethnic communities, more numerous, exert a kind of ostracism when the rap discourse does not carry the original problematic of rap (racial integration problems, defiance of law and order, quest for money, and seduction, among others).[1] At the same time, Montreal's groups like Rainmen, Royal Hill, Sans Pression, and Muzion are perceived, and are often presented as the sole representatives of rap in Quebec because they take into account crossbreed cultural forms that go beyond identity reclusion or the prerogatives of the demands by the social groups that represent the young people. From there, some atomized groups have started to appear in the suburbs and they claim a certain authenticity and autonomy by identifying themselves with the two first digits of their phone number: in Montreal, for example, 64 designates neighborhoods at the center of the city; in Quebec, 83 regroups a large section of the south bank. More and more, Quebec labels or independent ones endorse such a project by one or the other group of rap and they produce a record that most often does not survive long. Looking closely though, one can see that these groups are engaging themselves in a performing round where "the symbolic space of the cultural, social and artistic blend is validated by ethnicity more so than by diverse conflicting identifications" (Laplantine and Nouss, 302). In fact, the identity question is at the center of the discourse, but it is no more a question of national identity, as can be observed in more traditional types of songs, but rather a transcultural question, since one does not hesitate to express first or second generation ethnic origins by using his vernacular language mixed with French. For example, Muzion raps in Creole as well as in French and in English because these languages are part of his daily life. More so, one makes a statement of his long journey across a culture of adoption, a culture that very often opposes itself to the culture of origin and tends to operate a merging. Differing from rock or pop, which we associate easily with English language, rap represents a form of resistance against the globalization of economy and the uniformization of cultural identities. The compilation, *Berceau de l'Amérique* (America's Cradle), volumes 1 and 2, produced by Deux Faces-Le Gémeaux, clearly illustrates this shift toward a vastly more open discourse addressing cultural blends. At least ten groups now proclaim loudly their belonging to America, but to a Francophone and multiethnic America that rejects both American imperialism and linguistic and sociopolitical sectarianism. Yet, one must remember that this project is the initiative of white French-speakers and no group coming from an ethnic community has wanted to be associated with it. If rap and hip-hop cultures constitute the common territory of all Quebec groups that adhere to this musical movement, it is nevertheless a tacit agreement based on a cultural paradox that splits these groups into two distinct entities. In short, rap is a common musical space but it is divided into two separate territories. The one is characterized by white culture, the other by immigrant culture of newly arrived ethnic groups in Quebec.

THE SOCIAL FIELD AND THE MUSICAL FIELD: THE ROOTS OF A PARADOX

To understand the double dynamic of the social and musical fields in Quebec, we must analyze more closely the problematic of identity that prods Quebec's society in general. In effect, over roughly the last ten years, the question of Quebec identity has been submitted to a vast public debate that we can summarize in two main questions: Who is a Quebecer? How does one become a Quebecer? This debate has emerged since the referendum of 1991[2] after which some influential politicians lamented the homogeneity of the ethnic vote.[3] The foundations of Quebec identity have since fallen back into place without a satisfying evaluation of that problematic. For example, in literature, the designation "littérature migrante" (Migrating Literature), as imperfect as it is, allows perception of the new relation sustained by the indigenous literature toward the one now written by adopted Quebecers. This problematic favors the Other; that is, the immigrant communities that claim their own culture and identity and do not recognize themselves in the notion of *Quebecitude*, for this concept of Quebec identity rests primarily on French hereditary links that go back three centuries.

The social field thus permits the emergence of fierce exogenous voices, those which appropriate a certain musical substratum, rap in this case, and then develop a discourse acting directly on a consciousness of marginality. The musical field allows for the appearance of a paradox confronting Quebec identity, an identity represented in the rap produced and consumed by the white French community and another emerging from these "visible minorities," produced by people rupturing with ethnic homogeneity, but that is nevertheless listened to by those same white people. Now, if the paradox of the musical field is quite visible, the one associated with the musical scene is just as visible since white rap circulates freely in regions and in the periphery of large urban centers without getting its way to the very heart of artistic recognition which is Montreal. In other words, groups like Muzion, Rainmen, Royal Hill, and others reign over Montreal, the pre-eminent stay of rap in Quebec, but they fail to emerge outside of their domain. There was, for example, a hip-hop evening in Quebec that ended up in a fight between the white public and the rappers of color supported by their fans who had made the journey from Montreal to Quebec. This incident occurred on an old converted ferryboat cruising along the St. Lawrence River in front of Quebec City.

One can make a statement: white French rap groups do have their legitimacy and are recognized where the white population is predominant. However, where they represent a sub-product of a culture dominated by ethnic ascendance, they are confined to marginality and to parallel scenes. Moreover, this is the case everywhere there is a rap movement, be it in France, in English-Canada, or anywhere else. Rappers' authenticity is certified by their social differentiation. The hegemonic culture in those countries is white and either French or English and it is out of place with the very foundations of hip-hop culture claiming to be for the excluded. Rappers such as IAM, M.C. Solaar, Rascalz, and Choclair express the discourse of exclusion, the discourse of those not yet completely assimilated by the indigenous culture. They are *Beurs, pieds-noirs*,[4] Arabs, Jamaicans, Africans, Spanish, Amerindians, or crossbreeds and they openly reject any form of assimilation that would make them lose the roots of their identity. Thus, we are not surprised when their traditional music finds a way into their samplings.

In the preceding pages, I have analyzed the cultural paradox of rap made in Quebec, a paradox that stigmatizes ethnic heterogeneity more so than it achieves the conviviality that should characterize hip-hop culture. In this way, Quebec's hip-hop culture is marked by an excessive atomization that guarantees the survival of the rap movement in the musical field, while it multiplies the identity quest of those who fuel the movement. Quebec's rap is characterized by multiple entities defined in many ways (ethnic, social, and regional, to name but a few), which not only assures the vitality of the hip-hop movement but also sustains and cultivates the cultural and ethnic differences. In other words, the advent of the different ethnic, linguistic, and civil communities that make up Quebec's population nourishes a culture of paradox inside a cultural paradox.

NOTES

1. This ostracism stems from a latent racism at the base. For instance, a Wu Tan Klan show was postponed because some tracts had begun to circulate where it was written: "Rap is for Black People only, White People are forbidden."

2. In November 1991, Quebec's government held a referendum asking for a mandate to negotiate the sovereignty of Quebec and its association with the rest of Canada, together with the recognition of the distinct community status: 51% of the population voted against while 49% were in favor.

3. In the areas of high ethnic concentration, nearly 99% of the population voted against the referendum, in contrast to the areas where the majority was white and French and where the vote was evenly split.

4. Editor's note: The *pieds-noirs* are French nationals who settled and remained in the former French colonies of North Africa, especially Algeria, until these countries gained their independence in the 1960s.

WORKS CITED

Adams, John. "La musique rap." *Compositeur Canadien/Canadian Composer* Summer 1991: 18–19.

Anonymous. "Dubmatique, *La force de comprendre*." *Ici* 27 Nov.–4 Dec. 1997: 13.

———. "The Rascalz." *HHP* (Hip-Hop Connection) June 1997: 8.

Billy, Hélène de. "Rap around-the-clock." *L'Actualité* 15.1 (1990): n. pag.

Caudeiron, Daniel. "L'échantillonage." *Compositeur Canadien/Canadian Composer* Fall 1993: 12–13.

———. "Le maître du hip-hop." *Compositeur Canadien/Canadian Composer* Spring 1990: n. pag.

———. "Le Hip hop d'ici." *Compositeur Canadien/Canadian Composer* Nov. 1989: 30–35.

Caudeiron, Daniel, and Mark Miller. "Rap." *Encyclopédie de la Musique au Canada*. Montreal: Fides, 1993. 2855–57.

Desmond. "Rascalz." *Peace Magazine* Apr.–May 1997: 12.

Doole, Kerry. "The Maple Leaf Rap." *Music Express* 150 (1990): n. pag.

Galloway, Matt. "Toronto Rhymer Choclair Sweeter than All the Rest." *Now* Dec.–Jan. 1997: n. pag.

Gudino, Rod. "Rascalz Reap a Cash Crop." *RPM* 31 Mar. 1997: 8.

Jennings, Nicholas. "The Big Rap Attack." *Maclean's* 12 Nov. 1990: n. pag.

Kelly, Brendan. "Hip hop de chez nous." *Montreal Gazette* 25 Nov. 1997: F9.

Krims, Adam. *Rap Music and the Poetics of Identity*. Cambridge: Cambridge UP, 2000.

Laplantine, François, and Alexis Nouss. *Métissages: De Arcimboldo à Zombo*. Paris: Pauvert, 2001.

Litorco, Frank. "Second Coming, West Coast Style." *FFWD* 7 May 1997: 3.

Morales, Rigo. "Behold the Second Coming: Choclair." *The Source* June 1997: n. pag.

Nazareth, Errol. "Dragon Rap's Magic for Rascalz' Red 1." *The Toronto Sun* 16 May 1997: 5.

———. "La Musique Rap." *La Scène musicale/Musical Scene* 362 (1988): n. pag.

Quinlan, Thomas. "Rascalz, Elemental Journey." *Watch* Apr. 1997: 11.

———. "Rascalz, Cash Crop." *Watch* Mar. 1997: 10.

Philips, Colin. "World Play." *The Word* Apr. 1997: 5.

Rose, Tricia. *Black Noise, Rap Music and Black Culture in Contemporary America*. Hanover: Wesleyan UP, 1994.

Samuels, Allison, N'Gai Croal, and David Gates. "The Rap on Rap." *Newsweek* 9 Oct. 2000: 58–66.

DISCOGRAPHY

Bran Van 3000. *Glee*. Audiogram, 1997.

French B. *French B*. Sumo/Audiogram, 1991.

Choclair. *What It Takes*. Kneedeep Records, 1997.

Deux Faces-le Gémeaux. *Appelle-ça comme tu veux*. Tacca Musique, 1999.

Different Shades of Black. *Crazy Fiction*. Peanuts and Corn Records Family, 1994.

Dream Warriors. *And Now the Legacy Begins*. Island, 1991.

Dubmatique. *D*. Les Disques Tox, 1999.

——. *La force de comprendre*. Les Disques Tox, 1997.

Frek Sho. *Mocean*. Vagrant Hobby Records, 1997.

Haltown Projex. *Haltown Projex*. Jo-runs Records, 1996.

——. *Haltown 2*. Jo-runs Records, 1994.

——. *Haltown Junior*. Jo-runs Records, 1991.

H.D.V. *Sex, Drugs & Violence*. ISBA, 1991.

Kish. *Order from Chaos*. A&M, 1990.

K-OS (Kardinal Offishall). *Eye & I*. Capitol Hill Entertainment, 1997.

La Constellation. *Dualité*. Tacca Musique, 1997.

La Gamic. *La Gamic*. Les Disques Tox, 1998.

Laymen Twaist. *Walk on the Wild Side*. Isba, 1990.

Les Messagers du Son. *Les Messagers du Son*. Guy Cloutier Communications, 1997.

LMDS. *Il faudrait leur dire*. Guy Cloutier Communications, 1999.

——. *LMDS*. Guy Cloutier Communications, 1997.

Loco Locass. *Manifestif*. Audiogram, 2000.

M.O.S.T. *Black Charisme*. Select, 2000.

MCJ and Cool G. *So Listen*. Cap, 1990.

Maestro Fresh-Wes. *Symphony in Effect*. Attic, 1989.

Michie Mee and LA Luv. *Jamaican Funk-Canadian Style*. First Priority/Atlantic, 1991.

Mood Ruff. *Fluid*. Peanuts and Corn Records, 1996.

Morricone, Ennio. *Once Upon a Time in the West: The Original Soundtrack Recording*. BMG/RCA, 1989.

Muzion. *Mentalité Moune Morne*. VIK/BMG, 1999.

Rainmen. *Armageddon*. DEP/Radisson, 1999.

Rascalz. *Cash Crop*. Figure IV/BMG, 1997.

———. *Really Livin*. Figure IV/BMG, 1993.

Reed, Lou. *Walk on the Wild Side: The Best of Lou Reed*. RCA, 1988.

Royal Hill. *Atmosphères*. Ozone Records, 1998.

Salt-N-Pepa. *Blitz of Salt-N-Pepa Hits*. Polygram, 1992.

Shades of Culture. *Mindstate*. 2112 Records, 1998.

———. *Payin' Rent*. 2112 Records, 1997.

The Shuffle Demons. *Streetnicks*. Shuffle Demon Productions, 1986.

Social Deviantz. *Essential Mental Nutrients*. Sugarshack Records, 1997.

Swollen Members. *Swollen Members*. Battle Axe Records, 1997.

Taktika. *Mon mic, mon forty, mon blunt*. Explicit Productions, 2001.

Various Artists. *Berceau de l'Amérique II*. Explicit Production, 2001.

———. *Berceau de l'Amérique I*. Explicit Production, 2000.

———. *Beatfactory Rapessentials Volume Two*. Beatfactory/EMI, 1997.

———. *Chocolate Park (Compilation)*. Chocolate Park Entertainment, 1997.

———. *Beatfactory Rapessentials Volume One*. Beatfactory/EMI, 1996.

———. *Je rappe en français (compilation)*. Station 12, 1991.

———. *Cold Front (compilation)*. Attic, 1991.

Index

moonwalk, 101; ninety-nine, 101;
pointing, 101; popping, 101;
scorpion, 101; tetris, 101; thomas,
101; top-rock, 101; tracks, 101;
up-rock, 101; vogueing, 101
Dans la Rue la Danse, 103. *See also*
dance
Daoud, Zakya, 49, 50, 61n16
Das EFX, 38, 39
Davet, Stéphane, 46
Davis, Miles, xiii
Dee Nasty, 2, 4
Deleuze, Gilles, 94
Démocrates D, 6, 13
de Montvalon, Jean-Baptiste, 62n18
De Rudder, Véronique, 50, 61n14,
61n16
Desplanques, Guy, 61n14
Deux Faces-le Gémeaux, 131, 132
disco music, 1, 8
dj, dj-ing, vii, 1, 12, 13, 22, 39,
42n4, 74n4, 99, 130
DJ Nerve, 131
Doc Gynéco, 15
Dream Team Gathering, 39
Dream Warriors, 126, 127
Dr. Dre, 124
Dr. Frankenstein, 131
Druon, Maurice, 7
Dubet, François, 61n15, 69, 74n6
Dubmatique, 129
Dufresne, David, 57, 58
Durand, Alain-Philippe, x, xiii–xvii
Duret, Pascal, 56
Durkheim, Emile, 79

Earth, Wind, and Fire, xiii
Ebony Crew, 126
Egypt, 11, 29. *See also* Africa
Eleventh Reflektah, 131
Elias, Norbert, 84
EJM, 5
EMC, 13

Eminem, 5, 124
Expression Direkt, 15
Eye Spy Crew, 129

Fab 5 Freddy, 2, 62n21. *See also*
television channels and shows
Fabe, 13, 57
Fabulous Trobadors, 15
Faf Larage, 22–23, 29–30, 36–37, 129
Fang, 110–19, 121n2, 121n9,
121n10. *See also* Gabon
fans, 14, 33–44, 133
Fast J, 12
Fishman, Joshua, 122n13
folklore, 25

La Fonky Family, 22–23, 29–30, 35,
53
Fraction Hexagone, 46
Franklin, Aretha, xiii
free-style, 71, 104
French B, 128
The French Connection, *31n3. See
also* Marseilles
Front National (FN), 10, 11, 14, 25,
39, 45, 46, 59n4
Funk Attitude, 103. *See also* dance
funk(y), xiii, 15, 60n6, 130

Gabon, xvi, 106–23. *See also* Africa
Gainsbourg, Serge, 27
Galland, Olivier, 79
La Gamic, 130
gangs, 3, 45
gangsta rap, 9–10, 45–67
Gangstarr, 55
Les Garçons Bouchers, 1
Gasquet-Cyrus, Médéric, xv, 26,
121n4
Les Gens, 15
George, Nelson, xiii, xv, 15
ghettos, 4, 17, 55, 60n6, 68, 79, 125,
128, 130

About the Editor

Alain-Philippe Durand is assistant professor of French and film studies at the University of Rhode Island. Besides his interests in hip-hop and cinema, he specializes in the contemporary French novel. He has published essays on French and Latin American culture, literature, and music. He is the author of *Un Monde techno. Nouveaux espaces électroniques dans le roman des français années 1980 et 1990* (Weidler, forthcoming).

About the Contributors

Michelle Auzanneau is associate professor of linguistics at the University of Paris V–René Descartes. She specializes in the study of African languages and dialects and has published extensively in various journals, including *Cahiers d'Etudes Africaines*, *La Linguistique*, *Plurilinguismes*, and *Langage et société*. She is the author of *La parole vive du Poitou. Une étude sociolinguistique en milieu rural* (L'Harmattan, 1999).

Hugues Bazin is a graduate of the Ecole des Hautes Etudes en Sciences Sociales in anthropology and sociology and has been an independent scholar in the social sciences since 1993. He works primarily on the problematics of popular forms and emerging cultures. Following research conducted between 1990 and 1995, which yielded the book *La culture hip-hop* (Desclée de Brouwer, 1995), Bazin undertook a series of studies between 1995 and 2000 on artists in working-class neighborhoods.

Manuel Boucher is research professor at the Institute of Social Development in Rouen, France, where he directs the program Peoples and Cultures of Haute Normandie. His most recent publications include *Les théories de l'intégration. Entre universalisme et différentialisme* (L'Harmattan, 2000) and *Rap expression des lascars. Significations et enjeux du rap dans la société* (L'Harmattan, 1999).

Roger Chamberland is professor of literature at Laval University in Quebec. A specialist in the study of Quebecois songs and popular music, he has a strong interest in hip-hop culture. He directs the journal *Québec français* as well as a research group on music videos. He is the author of *Anthologie de la chanson québécoise* (Nuit Blanche, 1994) and coauthor of five volumes of the *Dictionnaire des oeuvres littéraires du Québec* (Fides, 1994). He contributed an essay to Tony Mitchell's *Global Noise: Rap and Hip-Hop Outside the USA* (Wesleyan UP, 2001) and he has published extensively on literature and popular music in various journals.

Lars Erickson (translator) is assistant professor of French at the University of Rhode Island. He has written and published on various topics relating to the French Enlightenment. His book *Metafact: Essayistic Science in Eighteenth-Century France* (North Carolina Studies in the Romance Languages and Literatures, forthcoming) examines literature's role in the emergence of modern science.

Anne-Marie Green is professor of sociology at the University of Besançon and the University of Paris—Sorbonne. She is also the director of F.M.O. (French Musical Observatory) at the Sorbonne, where for the last fifteen years her research has concentrated primarily on the meaning of music and its impact on contemporary society. She is the author of *Musique et sociologie. Enjeux méthodologiques et approches empiriques* (L'Harmattan, 2000), *Musicien de métro. Approche des musiques vivantes urbaines* (L'Harmattan, 1998), and *Des jeunes et des musiques. Rock, Rap, Techno* (L'Harmattan, 1997).

Jean-Marie Jacono is associate professor of music at the University of Provence in Aix-en-Provence. His research interests include rap music, Russian opera, and the sociology of music. He contributed chapters to *Existential Semiotics* (Indiana UP, 2001), *Paroles et musiques à Marseille— Les voix d'une ville* (L'Harmattan, 1999), and *La Musique depuis 1945— Matériau, Esthétique et Perception* (Mardaga, 1996).

Adam Krims is associate professor of music and director of the Institute for Popular Music at the University of Alberta. Author of *Rap Music and the Poetics of Identity* (Cambridge UP, 2000) and editor of

Music/Ideology: Resisting the Aesthetic (G + B Arts International, 1998), he has published numerous essays and articles on music, Marxism, urban geography, and cultural theory.

Alain Milon is professor of sociology at the University of Paris X–Nanterre. He collaborates with the research institute CITTAL as head sociologist, and he is a member of the Observatory of Graffiti in Paris. His recent publications include *L'étranger dans la Ville: Du rap au graff mural* (PUF, 1999), *L'art de la conversation* (PUF, 1999), and *La valeur de l'information: de la dette au don* (PUF, 1999).

Yannick Nassoy (translator) is a graduate of the Ecole Normale Supérieure in Lyon. He defended a Master's thesis in 2000 entitled *Translation of* Where you'll find me *by Ann Beattie, Followed by a Study of English Nominalization and of Their Translation into French*.

Anthony Pecqueux teaches at the University of Avignon et des Pays de Vaucluse and is a doctoral student at the Ecole des Hautes Etudes en Sciences Sociales (EHESS) in Marseilles. He is the author of a thesis entitled *Le rap public à l'épreuve sérieuse des institutions et nonchalante de ses publics. Contribution à une socio-anthropologie du rap* (2000).

The late **André J. M. Prévos** was associate professor of French at Pennsylvania State University–Worthington Scranton Campus, and associate editor of the *Encyclopedia of Popular Music of the World*. He has published extensively on popular French music in publications such as *The French Review*, *Popular Music and Society*, and *Contemporary French Civilization*. He will be missed by scholars, colleagues, and friends alike.

Paul Rogers (translator) is a doctoral student at the University of North Carolina at Chapel Hill. He studies medieval French literature and wrote his Master's thesis in 1998 on a play of an Ivory Coast playwright, Bernard Zadi Zaourou.

Ralph Schoolcraft (translator) is assistant professor of French at Texas A&M University–College Station. He has written *Romain Gary: The*

Man Who Sold His Shadow (UPenn Press, 2002) and has translated Henry Rousso, *The Haunting Past: History, Memory and Justice in Contemporary France* (UPenn Press, 2001). He is currently completing *Literary Gaullism: Representations of the French Resistance*.

Paul A. Silverstein is assistant professor of anthropology at Reed College. His research on the transnational political culture of Algerians in France has been published in *Social Text, Middle East Report, Migrations-Société*, and various edited collections. He is currently finishing a manuscript entitled *Trans-Politics: Islam, Berberity, and the French Nation-State*.

Seth Whidden (translator) is assistant professor of French at the University of Missouri–Columbia. A specialist in nineteenth-century French poetry, he has published articles on Rimbaud, Verlaine, and Marie Krysinska, and has translated Krysinska's short story "Ingénuité: Moeurs américaines" for the volume *Nineteenth-Century Women Seeking Expression: Translations from the French*. His critical edition of Krysinska's *Rythmes pittoresques* (1890) will be published by the "Textes littéraires" series of the University of Exeter Press in 2002.

Mary-Angela Willis (translator) is lecturer of French at the University of Rhode Island. She completed a Ph.D. in Francophone literature at the University of Alabama in 2001. Her research interests include Mashreq and Maghreb literatures and postcolonial literature and gender studies, in particular women's literature on conflict and war.